SC1-

c. 2004
2X 11/04 · 12/04
5X 4/10 2/11

OCT 2 6 2004

FACE IT

Recognizing and Conquering the
Hidden Fear
That Drives All Conflict at Work

Art Horn

American Management Association

New York • Atlanta • Brussels • Chicago • Mexico City • San Francisco
Shanghai • Tokyo • Toronto • Washington, D.C.

Special discounts on bulk quantities of AMACOM books are available to corporations, professional associations, and other organizations. For details, contact Special Sales Department, AMACOM, a division of American Management Association, 1601 Broadway, New York, NY 10019.
Tel.: 212-903-8316. Fax: 212-903-8083.
Web site: www.amacombooks.org

Library of Congress Cataloging-in-Publication Data

Horn, Art, 1954–
    Face it : recognizing and conquering the hidden fear that drives all conflict at work / Art Horn.
        p.   cm.
    Includes bibliographical references and index.
    ISBN 0-8144-0835-4 (hardcover)
    1. Psychology, Industrial. 2. Employees—Psychology. 3. Conflict management. 4. Interpersonal relations. I. Title.

HF5548.8.H63 2004
650.1'3—dc22

                                                    2004001813

Printing number

10   9   8   7   6   5   4   3   2   1

To my kids, their kids, and all the kids thereafter.
This is what the old man thought.

Contents

Preface

This book began life as a letter to my children. Like a will, it was to be one of those documents one leaves behind for others to read after the writer has passed away. Its purpose was to explain what I thought about some of the big issues: meaning, purpose, mental health, reading people, surviving loss. I added ruminations to the letter while on flights between speaking engagements, when there was ample time to organize my thoughts. After a few years of this, the letter was getting awfully long. It was time to change formats. Hence, this book.

I must first of all thank my wife, Joan Berman. She read and reacted to the first draft of each chapter while it was still warm from my printer. Her insight is present everywhere in these pages, and her unconditional love has enabled me to be me.

Two close friends—Les Lear and Dr. Arnie Ein—have also contributed to this book, in more ways than one. Aside from receiving specific feedback from them, I have learned from them both, each in their own way, much about myself, humanity, and humility.

I am deeply grateful to my colleagues. We banter back and forth about many of the ideas in this book on a daily basis. I must mention by name David Batchelor, Barbara Gaiptman, Lisa Tomassetti, and Sean Verhoeven; as members of our company's senior leadership team, these are the people I interact with most frequently and so learn from. But everyone in my organization—including those who are no longer part of the team—has contributed.

I probably learn the most from the people I coach. Every single person is different. The challenges they face may be similar to those of others I have seen, but I am consistently and pleasantly surprised by differences in nuance. I walk into a coaching session with a model in my head for how I think people tick, and I finish that session with a slightly improved model. I receive a gift from every hour with every client.

Speaking of those clients, the privacy of each and every one of them described in this book has been painstakingly protected. Names, titles, and industries have been changed so that nobody could know who in the real world is being described. Even the stories of the progress of coaching dialogues and relationships have been modified in order to conceal identities. For example, if I report that Willie said two things, then in real life somebody other than Willie said one of the two things and somebody else said the other.

I will not, however, conceal my own identity as the client of my therapists. Dr. John Weiser and Patricia Kirby worked hard over the years to support my growth and delicately offered their wisdom at exactly the right times. In addition, my thanks to Paula, who was my first meditation teacher. We have not been in contact for over twenty-five years, but I know she's out there. She introduced me to the possibility of meditative transcendence. John McLeod, an old friend, helped me organize my thoughts on innumerable occasions over the years. My in-laws, Gertrude and Aaron Berman, merit mention as well: They have created a secure family context, forming a solid foundation for everyone around them, including me.

Last, but only to end on a high note, I am immeasurably indebted to my editor, Don Bastian. Don helped to scope out the book and find a publisher. During the writing phase, he cleaned up my messes, demanded greater clarity, challenged my thoughts, encouraged me when I needed it, and ably handled things behind the scenes. It is a fact that if it were not for Don, you would not have this book in your hand.

Introduction

Face it. As negative as it may sound, fear is a pretty big player in the business world. We try to be positive, we talk about confidence and the need for a positive attitude, but even if we've got things under control ourselves, many people around us seem to be wrestling with their fears much of the time.

Fear shows up in many ways in business.

Think about the people who work around you. Perhaps you know someone who is afraid of confrontation, so she never addresses problems with people head on. You may have a colleague in sales who is reluctant to cold call or nail down customer commitments because of a core fear of rejection. His sales volume isn't as high as he knows it could be. Maybe you know a leader whose fear of failure holds him back from taking risks. Forward momentum in his organization is stifled. Most offices have at least one employee who is so afraid of being judged negatively that silence is their norm. Coworkers don't get access to the intelligence available to them.

All these situations are ripe for conflict as people hide from each other, aggress against each other, misunderstand each other, miscommunicate with each other. Besides hurting their own careers and the careers of those around them, they are limiting the success of their organizations and, unfortunately, limiting the harmony of their relationships outside work. There is no doubt that fear is a common obstacle to personal and organizational success. The characteristics of the worriers, controllers, fakes, and other quintessential business types described in the first part of this book can all be traced to fear. They are the people I see most frequently in my coaching practice. The presence of fear as the core driver of their patterned behavior has emerged loud and clear. And I have seen the aforementioned conflict decrease markedly as they have owned their fear and worked through their problems.

The Patterns

Wouldn't it be great to understand these fear-driven patterns? This book offers a big step in gaining that understanding, helping you to understand your own patterns and helping you to get along better with people who exhibit these patterns. Throughout this book we will look closely at how to transcend these ways of acting and free ourselves from the troublesome feelings that accompany them.

No, I am not trying to pull you into a literary psychotherapy session. I am not a therapist, though I have had my fair share of therapy and have studied the therapeutic process. My training is mostly in philosophy. Philosophers think about ideas. They use reason to sort things out. More specifically, I am an executive coach. I spend a good deal of my time talking to people one-on-one about their business challenges, usually as they relate to feeling good about themselves on the job or interacting effectively with other people.

I've been coaching for twenty years. Through those years, I have been engaged to apply philosophical thinking to help people sort out people-related problems on the job. I have seen patterns in how clients behave under certain circumstances. Along the way I have researched the work of various thinkers in order to understand what I was seeing. I have as-similated, massaged, and applied a simple model to explain how people tend to operate. As you'll see, this model, which I call the Transcendence Model, is very useful and effective.

Insecurity

The Transcendence Model will be explained several times throughout the book. Each time we will approach the matter from a different angle. But here's the basic explanation. You exist. You have wants. Often other people and various facts of life are in the way. That's a problem. So, there is the possibility of insecurity. Insecurity is a part of what it is to be human. You might say it's built right into the fabric of life itself. I coached some-one recently who said, "Ah, so we want to make love with the universe, and we just can't." "Right," I said, "so we're left with this lifetime sense of disunity. And it's very frustrating."

We fight this frustration, this insecurity. When we are reminded of it, we experience some level of angst. Many of us spend our lives moving away from our insecurity. Certainly the controller seeks to get what she wants, lest she must face it. The worrier fears it. The fake hides it. So does the victim. The attention-seeker tries to fill the hole created by it. As you can see, lots of people are engaged in a busy dynamic around the matter.

Is this a new discovery? Not at all. Although this book is not about Buddhism, and I am not a Buddhist, there are millions of practitioners of this religion who operate on the assumption that "life is suffering." And millions of people have read thousands of nonreligious self-help books that espouse a similar view. It was the psychologist Eric Fromm who wrote, in the 1960s, that once we leave our mother's womb, we experience aloneness and separateness for the first time, and we suffer from it for the rest of our lives. (And, as one comedian has put it, we spend the rest of our lives trying to get back in.)

We're all insecure. So what? Is the explanation an oversimplification? Yes. In fact, if it's true of everyone, there may not be a lot of value in making the claim. But the model's true value comes from its use as a tool to explain certain behaviors and to direct our attention to some basic guidelines. Yes, we're all insecure. We all feel angst when our stability is in question. When we experience insecurity, we seem to get lost in it. In a sense, we "become" it. We identify ourselves with it. From that point of view, we don't usually see our way out of it. But by tracing it back to a simple source, and then by following the guideline that we must accept that particular angst as a part of our lives, and working at that acceptance, we feel relief. We also get one step closer to being able to preempt and move beyond the same stimulus/response dynamic in the future. This is transcendence.

Coaching vs. Therapy

"Wait!" you might be thinking. "You're talking about therapy, not coaching!" Well, this is my kind of coaching. For me, coaching is a little faster than therapy. It's a little more direct. The coach is more likely to explain her view of what's happening than a therapist is. More than one client has said that having a coach is like having a philosophical therapist who understands the work environment. Others have described being coached as being subjected to philosophical scrutiny instead of therapeutic compassion. For many, I am simply a sounding board. But in all cases, I apply the Transcendence Model, because it is a proven guide for moving people to a better place.

As a coach, I try to get people to see the link between what they complain about and their fears and insecurities. I help clients to build that awareness so that they can begin to make different choices. I also help clients to process their emotions. Those two things, building an awareness of underlying feelings and processing feelings, elevate a person's ability to change.

I don't deal with certain problems that psychotherapists and other practitioners address. For example, I don't treat clinical depression, obsessive-compulsive behavior, or the experience of being haunted by an extremely traumatic event from the past. My focus is on the day-to-day problems of the average person in the workplace.

People come to me because they have challenging jobs and sometimes their behavior gets them into some kind of trouble, either in their own heads or in the opinions of other people. Worriers, for example, are personally tormented by their tendencies, yet their colleagues may not even know of their plight. Victims, on the other hand, usually frustrate other people with their tendency to deflect blame. They are often steered my way by their senior colleagues. Different still are attention-seekers. They don't come to me seeking help with their tendencies. They come for other reasons that happen to link to their tendencies, and they end up resolving both.

Business Pressures

It is a cliché to say life in contemporary organizations is tough. But clichés are usually true! Most of us have more to do than can be done. We have information blasting at us from multiple sources. There's workplace politics, the constant pressure to become more productive, increased marketplace threats. We must juggle these things in a world fraught with tension. And then, on top of all that, as individuals we are pressured to find balance between work and the rest of our lives.

I feel these pressures myself. In addition to being a coach, I run a training and consulting company that works with sales forces and management teams. For the first fifteen of our twenty years in business I was one of our facilitators. My job was to stand in front of small and large groups of people and facilitate discussion about leadership, coaching, and selling. I learned a lot about the challenges businesspeople face. I learned about the kind of outlook one needs in order to be optimally effective in these roles. And I learned how difficult it is to sustain this outlook.

When 9/11 hit, I found that my clients were more fearful than ever. I was, too. My company's flow of new sales stopped. I remember waiting for days for customers to start buying again. A whole new array of fears had arisen, the most selfish being that I was afraid of the possible demise of my own business. At the time when I most needed clarity and will and vision, I was least able to find it. I had to coach myself through it. I had to remind myself that my own fears were shutting me down. The simple statement running through my mind was, "I've got a problem." I was afraid. I knew I had to get in touch with my fear in order to tame it. I had to "own" my fear, meaning, as we'll see later, that I had to acknowledge that I possess and will always possess a fearful little boy inside me. By connecting with this little boy, I was able to connect what I was experiencing regarding my company's survival with my central fear of not being okay.

From Fear to Freedom

It's a beautiful thing. In owning our worst fears, acknowledging that they are a part of us, we tame them. The irony is that accepting fear as part of you means being less driven by that fear. This book will help you move from this kind of fear to this kind of freedom.

Part I of this book, The People in Your Neighborhood, considers the makeup of six business types: the *worrier*, the *controller*, the *fake*, the *attention-seeker*, the *victim*, and the *prisoner*. Using case histories, we will explore each type in detail. Chances are, you work for or with several of these types. Or you are one of them yourself. One thing you will notice is that each of the people referred to in the book made dramatic strides in effectiveness when they learned to accept themselves.

Part II, Hell Is Not Just Other People, explores the Transcendence

Model in detail. The problem is not just outside us—the people we work with—but often is inside us. We'll see how we spend so much of our time assessing whether we like what we see in our lives—our jobs, the people around us, the politics, the media, the physical world. And we'll define the role of that assessment in the various emotions that drive us. This involves looking at the distinction between two types of thoughts. We have thoughts about the facts of the world—such as that you are reading this sentence right now—and we have opinions about those facts. A key point we'll play with is that life is so much sweeter when we place our attention on the facts and resist the temptation to reach our opinions. We will wrestle with the pressure to reach opinions in our jobs even though the opinions get us into personal and professional trouble. We'll learn about the need to strike a balance between these opposing positions.

The main topic of the final section of this book—Part III, Moving from Fear to Freedom—is your ongoing progress. We will talk about your personal thinking patterns as they relate to patterns in your emotional responses and behaviors relating to the types in this book. We'll label your personal pattern your *operating strategy*, the way you evaluate things in your life and how you personally respond to your evaluations.

Processing your feelings is a key component of this part of the book. This might feel like the hard stuff. You'll discover how your experience of who you are in any given moment intimately links to whatever is crossing your mind. If you are angry, then you, well, *are* angry. You "become" whatever crosses your mind. A goal might be for you to become the possessor of your feelings rather than the feelings themselves. We'll look at how you can make such a shift.

Of course, if feelings come from the judgments we make, and one goal is to resolve feelings, it makes good sense to learn about how to stop judging ourselves. We will also consider means to stop judging others, since many people—and workplaces—get into trouble based on habits related to this behavior.

Another focus of this part of the book is the nature of personal commitment. You will see how learning about your operating strategy, processing your feelings more effectively, and learning to preempt certain emotional responses before getting hooked by them opens you up to the possibility of significantly improved "willpower" and capacity to commit.

In the final chapters of the book we will look at operating in a place where you are free of harmful thinking habits and can even experience optimal human happiness. We will also explore the topic of living with personal transcendence.

If you think of one of the most impressive and effective business-people you know, that person probably is in touch with whoever is in her presence in an attentive and compassionate way; she is very focused on achieving targets and is very intentional; and she is not inclined to blame but rather seeks solutions and appropriate action. A major thesis of this book is that this mind-set can be created and sustained.

Working and living in a place of personal transcendence implies we are holding judgment in abeyance, so we are not involved in blaming. We have a sense of where we want to go, as opposed to our fear of failure blocking the dream. We take responsibility for getting there, as opposed to fearing the blame for not having already arrived. We have confidence in our ability to achieve the goal, as opposed to letting our fears deplete our conviction. We have the ability to set our ego aside so that we can listen to the input of others, as opposed to having to hide our true self because of our fears of being found out.

I am convinced that if there is such a thing as "enlightenment" for those of us in the business world, it emanates from transcending the struggles of ego and simply staying focused on the job at hand. It is worry free, empowering, and of clear conscience. Yes, it is hard work to achieve this, but it is well within reach. It is very personal, but only for a while. It certainly helps get the job done. Free of politics around us and, in a sense, within us, there's even time to spare for balance in our lives.

PART I

The People
in Your
Neighborhood

CHAPTER 1

The Worrier

Most of us worry a bit. When times are tough and we don't know how things are going to work out, we feel some level of anxiety. This is a normal response.

For some of us, however, the anxiety is problematic. Worry can be quite self-defeating. When it strikes, we think something unfortunate might happen. Often dealing with the unfortunate matter requires clarity, and this is exactly what worrying destroys. As a result, on-the-job worry reduces productivity. It also usually affects the employee's family life and sense of personal satisfaction.

People who call themselves "worriers" know they have a problem. Interestingly, some report that when they don't feel worried, they take it as a sign that they are missing something. So they worry about it. Other worriers worry about their worry. That's where a coach can help.

Hartley, the owner of an audiovisual services company, had been a worrier all of his forty-year-old life. He came to me preoccupied with the challenge faced by many owners of small businesses: cash flow. He had twenty employees. Some of his clients didn't pay their bills on time, and he had an inadequate line of credit at the bank. He lived with the worry of making payroll every two weeks and keeping his business afloat.

Hartley acknowledged that his personal spending habits were part of his problem. He would take more money out of the company than he could afford. But he had deep needs around maintaining a high standard of living for his family of six.

Of course, at a practical level, he could have solved his problem by spending less and building a savings pool that could act as a line of credit for times when sales were low or when late payments by clients threatened his payroll. But that was not so easy. Hartley couldn't seem to save any money.

"I can't just start saving now," he told me. "My regular payments at home are locked in. I've got two car leases, a huge mortgage, insurance costs like you wouldn't believe. Cutting down on groceries and long-distance calls would be trivial and would just frighten my wife."

Although he was always worried about money problems, Hartley made it clear he hadn't come to me for financial advice. "The fact is, I've been in business for eleven years and nothing has really changed," he said. "I do have a constant cash flow problem but I always get through it. What I want help with is the worrying I seem to be doing all the time."

It was debatable whether we could separate his money problems from his worry problem, but I had no problem starting with his chronic worrying.

I asked him to verbalize the kinds of thoughts that go on in his head when he's in bed at night, sleepless with worry. He closed his eyes and attempted to let the feelings fly.

"Well, let's say I was thinking of having to call Bill, a customer, about the dates on some project. I might think, 'Oh, yeah, Bill still has that unpaid invoice from the previous job we did for him . . . says it wouldn't go through their accounts payable system because the receipts weren't attached. It's not fair. If he sits on it, and we don't get that check from Dumont, there won't be enough for payroll again. We'll be $11,000 short. And the line of credit is already tapped out. And it'll take me weeks to get backup receipts. Dumont always pays late. I need more clients. But I can't ask Jim, my sales rep, to cold call. He's a wimp. I can't rely on anybody. But if I pressure Jim, he might leave. Then I'd have a huge problem. He could steal clients. Gotta keep Jim happy . . .'"

I could see tension in Hartley's face. He was wincing. He looked at me as if to say, "See?" I asked him where he felt the tension.

"It's a tightness in my chest," he replied. "I get it there all the time. It's stress."

There were telltale patterns in Hartley's demonstration. First, his physiology registered his stress and fear, which is understandable since, obviously, worry is linked to fear. The thoughts may come from the thinking part of the brain, the neocortex. But the feelings that accompany the thoughts come from the amygdala, the part of the brain responsible for core feelings like fear.

I also noticed the essential "what if . . ." construction of his thinking. That's what worriers tend to do: Their thoughts move from one vulnerability to another as they paint themselves into a fretful corner. Even if they set the conscious thinking about the problem aside, they still experience an undercurrent of anguish.

Hartley exhibited yet another defining characteristic of the worrier: a future orientation. Worry is about feeling uneasy in anticipation of things that might happen.

Why Worry?

Throughout this first part of the book, I'm going to assume that you are, to some degree or other, the business type I am discussing. Even if you're not, the analysis and advice below will help you understand and work with these types and deal with friends and family members struck with these problems. In addition, I end each chapter on these types with tips you might want to follow if you do work with the business type.

So let's assume that you are a worrier. A little bit of worry is normal and healthy. Our brains are built to help us avoid problems by worrying. A thought crosses our mind about a potential problem and we experience just enough fear to motivate us to produce a plan for addressing the problem. If we humans didn't have this motivation, we might not have survived as a species. The capacity to worry is genetic. The tendency to worry excessively is thought by some researchers to be genetic as well.

There are other explanations for why you may be a worrier. Like most worriers you may have learned to worry during your childhood. Parents may have role modeled worry and you just picked it up as a means of responding to problems. But it doesn't have to have originated during childhood. When stress levels rise, those predisposed to worry are more likely to become anxious and find themselves worrying. A pattern of worry can continue for years until their lives stabilize and they are less insecure.

People who seek help for worry fall into two categories: those who suffer from "normal anxiety," worry triggered by specific things, and those who suffer from "free-floating anxiety," worry that doesn't need a trigger and is pretty much always there. My coaching practice only serves the former group. These are people who find that the fear they experience when they worry is more intense or prolonged than a situation calls for. I refer the other worriers—those with free-floating anxiety—to psychotherapists, psychologists, or family doctors, for more intensive help.

Individuals usually report two or three themes that set them off, but there are as many triggers as there are worriers in the world. Money is a common subject of worry. So are physical health and the well-being of loved ones. Fears of confrontation, failure, and even success can also provoke an undesired worry response.

The original meaning of the verb *to worry* is "to gnaw." A dog "worries" a favorite bone. It chews the bone for a while, buries it, and digs it up later for yet another chew. Over and over again.

Have you ever had the experience of "it hurts so good"? Someone once told me that he could poke away at certain spots on his gums with a toothpick and get a kind of painful pleasure. My own gums don't respond quite that way, but I suppose it's possible. Of course, we've all heard of the sexual equivalent of the phenomenon. This is not to say that people actually get conscious pleasure from worry. They don't. But there can be at least four paybacks from worrying.

First, worrying may give a certain kind of pleasure that you are getting to the nub of a problem. A worrier finds herself tugged by her fear and feels that staying on the case will somehow resolve it. She feels she cannot let go of her worry just in case the worst-case scenario happens and the thing feared actually does rear its ugly head. If you ask a worrier why she worries, she will probably say that she is afraid a certain problem will arise. If you point out that nothing can be done about the problem so it's not worth the emotional investment, the worrier will report that she just can't stop it. There is a bad thing out there and it can't be ignored.

Second, worry may actually help solve a problem. Worriers sometimes do generate a solution to a problem by worrying about it, anticipating worst possible scenarios, and planning effective responses to all of them. Of course, the discomfort of the fear is not part of the worrier's equation—but so be it.

Third, worrying can be stimulating for some worriers. They bemoan the accompanying angst, but at some level there is a return on their investment. These people feel more alive when they are worrying about things. It's almost as if it makes them feel important. They may regret their worrying, but they don't really want to stop.

Fourth, worrying can pay off in the attention it draws from other people. When worriers express their concerns, coworkers, friends, and loved ones fall into a routine of soothing the pain. Ironically, they only make things worse. Sometimes these people fuel the pattern of worry by helping. Other times they fuel it by not helping, once they become wise to the worrier's patterns.

In spite of these paybacks, however, most worriers know their worrying isn't doing them any good.

Putting a Stop to Worry

Here are three different recommendations for you to help you stop worrying—and sometimes all three are required:

1. Develop practical tools for protecting against worry and its effects. For example, simply talking to someone can help you get certain fears off your chest. Often worriers keep things in because they are afraid to reveal their vulnerability. When you do reveal what's on your mind, you will tend to relax.

2. Embrace the fear. This can be challenging. The raw emotion of fear is beneath all the thoughts that you are churning over in your head. When you are worried, you are basically fearful. What can help is shining a light on that fear—uncovering its origin and ultimately embracing it as part of yourself. Ironically, embracing the fear will tend to allay it. Denying your fear tends to exaggerate it, as though your worry is a voice that will cry louder and louder until it feels it is being heard.

3. Work at enhancing your self-esteem. When you have high self-esteem, you tend to worry less. You are more likely to have faith in your ability to deal with life's challenges. The bad news is that the impulse to worry will still arise. We never say good-bye to this impulse. But the good news is that with high self-esteem there can be a remarkable decrease in the amount and severity of the worrying.

Let's look at each of these three approaches in more detail.

Developing Practical Tools

Various chemicals can relieve the anxiety that fuels, and results from, worry. On the undesirable side are alcohol and other recreational drugs. Though habit forming and therefore very risky, alcohol has been used by many over the ages to "take the edge off" the effects of worry. I don't recommend it. My first formal psychotherapeutic instructor started off the first class of a course by explaining how he used alcohol to self-medicate against the daily stresses of his life. He used the story to tell us that he was a recovering alcoholic.

More desirably, various selective serotonin reuptake inhibitors (SSRIs)—such as Prozac, Zoloft, and Paxil—have become commonplace due to their apparently profound effects on mood. Hundreds of thousands of patients have been helped courtesy of these medicines. They can be very useful to take during the course of a talk-therapy process. Of course, they require a doctor's prescription. Some people are reluctant to use these medicines and prefer a nonmedicinal approach. Here are six nonmedicinal practices that can help worriers.

Diversion

The first is diversion. Most worriers employ it already, and sometimes, if the object of worry is not too great, and if the worrier's self-esteem is high enough, it works like a charm. This technique is simple: Change the subject. Go do something different. Get your attention off the thing you are worrying about.

Diversion can be a little tricky, however. The very nature of worry is such that a worrier wants to keep worrying. The object of worry is like a magnet. For a worrier, the idea of choosing to attend to some other matter can be counterintuitive.

Diversion is a kind of thought-suppression technique, but, as the psychologist Daniel Wegner has written, thought suppression has a certain self-defeating tendency. The part of our consciousness that would seek to detect and veer away from worry could actually stimulate it instead. People do indeed have an ability to keep an eye out for things while they are otherwise occupied. For example, a parent can be at the kitchen table immersed in conversation while still watching a child. Similarly, we can keep an eye out for worrisome thoughts. The oddity is that when it comes to thought suppression, the part that is "keeping an eye out" happens to be so powerful that it actually reminds us that we are on guard against the worrisome thoughts. So, it's not easy to simply choose not to worry. The answer is to distract ourselves without trying too hard.

Action Plans

Another practical tool is to write an action plan. One of the stressful aspects of worry is that, by definition, we are not in control of the worrisome situation. After all, if we had control of a matter, we wouldn't have to worry about it. Making an action plan works because it gives the feeling of getting things under control. When you worry during a sleepless night, get out of bed and devise a strategy. Make a list of everything that's problematic about the worrisome matter, and for each item on the list decide on a countermeasure. Do this until you have effective countermeasures for all the anticipated eventualities.

Self-Reinforcement

Making action plans is even more effective when coupled with some self-reinforcement. For example, after you have set an action plan, tell yourself, "Okay, things are under control. If any of these bad things happens, I have a plan for it." When repeated out loud, this simple reframing of your outlook can nip the next worry episode in the bud. Saying things out loud to yourself (in private, to avoid having to worry about other people's impressions) can help you manage yourself.

Goals

Sometimes worriers feel unsettled because they have an important, unanswered question. I've heard clients ask things like: "Should I complain about my boss?" or "Should I pursue that job opportunity?" or "Should I tell my colleague what I really think?" They perceive a "damned if you do, damned if you don't" conflict. A solution can often be found in the effort to set goals. In a way, this is a form of diversion. When you are thinking about your goals, and determining ways to implement them, you are distracted from worrying about them. You also may end up eliminating the source of worry.

Rationalization

Most worriers know from experience with loved ones who are trying to help that there are some natural questions one can ask that can nudge them off of worry. The basic question to ask yourself is: "If the thing I am worried about actually happened, would things work out?" The predictable answer is usually yes, in the long run, things would work out. Although subjecting one's worries to rational inquisition really misses the point of fear-based worry, in certain cases, it can make a difference.

Worry Times

A surprisingly useful tool for managing day-to-day worry can be to arrange a specific time to fret. For example, you can set from 4:00 P.M. to 5:00 P.M. as your daily worry time. At the assigned time, go ahead, worry away. Go for it. But when the temptation arises at some other time, give yourself permission to save the rumination for the scheduled worry period. You can address the issue that provoked the worry impulse, but set aside the actual angst for later. After a few weeks of this approach, you may find that you worry less than when you started this new personal policy.

Embracing the Fear

For many, worry stems from a long-buried pain. One way to stop the worry is to feel the pain wholly. It can be a difficult journey, but the power of embracing that pain, of bringing it into the light of awareness, can work absolute wonders in changing a worrier's self-control.

In one sense, the notion of coming to grips with your hidden fear is simple. The idea is that regardless of the thing that's making you worried, underneath the surface is an unresolved fear. By isolating that fear, examining it a bit, acknowledging that it is a part of you, you will be more in control of your worry.

The real challenge, however, is in allowing yourself to experience it. Recall that Hartley was clear that there were two aspects to his situation: the tangible business problems, and the emotions that accompanied them. Hartley wanted to deal with the emotional aspects. He astutely resisted the temptation to blame the outside world for his problem. He knew that his business problems could be resolved, but he wasn't so sure about the vulnerability inside himself. He knew that others in exactly the same circumstances might not be so worried. He owned his own worry.

In our third session together I asked Hartley what he was afraid of.

"I'm afraid I won't be able to make payroll," he said.

"Okay," I replied, "and what would happen then?"

"Well, people would be mad at me and I would feel just terrible."

"What would be terrible?"

Hartley winced and tightened his shoulders. "They would be mad. I could go bankrupt."

"And what would happen then?"

"Well, I would disappoint my wife and my kids and my employees. It would be horrible."

I had to nudge him along. "Tell me more."

"I would feel worthless! It would hurt."

Now he was getting to the nub of it. He was locating the fear. "My world would be falling apart," he said. "I would feel so empty. So alone."

Hartley began to cry. He was a little embarrassed about crying in front of me, which was too bad, because a good cry was exactly what he needed.

I asked him what that hurt reminded him of. He paused for a minute or so, but that was okay because it was a big moment. He said he remembered being in his early teens sitting in the living room of his family home with his parents. His mother was sitting in a chair, upset, and Hartley was sitting at her feet feeling terrible. His father sat in another chair with his head in his hands.

"Why did you feel so hurt in that situation?" I asked.

"Because my world was falling apart. My mother was declaring that she was going to leave, and my father was helpless to step in and say what had to be said."

"What happened next?"

Hartley began to cry again. This time he could not hold it in. He explained, "I begged her not to leave. I had to beg her. And she got up and left anyway. She left. My world was falling apart. I tried to keep it together. I hated that moment. I still hate that moment! I cried so hard. My mommy was leaving me!"

I let him have another good cry. It gave him relief. When things calmed down, he was able to connect the dots between his current worry over business matters and the fear that he felt when his mother left him. For him, there was a direct link. As a young teen in his living room that day, he felt his world was falling apart; as a mature adult, he was carrying with him the constant fear that his world was going to fall apart.

That single occurrence was not the sole cause of Hartley's worry. As our relationship went on, I learned that he had been exposed at a young age to multiple fear provocations. He interpreted each of them as reminders that things can easily come unglued.

This is indeed how things work sometimes. When a person experiences hurt, the nervous system builds a defense to avoid a recurrence of the hurt. Needless to say, this programming in the brain has served the species well. By learning to avoid things that cause us problems, we increase our chances of survival.

Hartley's system was doing what it was automatically programmed to do: defending him against that hurt. As an adult, when he saw situations that could devolve into his world falling apart, a healthy fear stepped in. It was trying to warn him to avoid this problem at all costs. The regrettable part is that though the mechanism is healthy insofar as it is doing its job, it is also mistaken. It is a little hypersensitive. The fear pattern was understandable, given the pain that he was seeking to avoid. But it was not really serving him well.

By increasing his awareness of the direct link between his childhood and his worry, Hartley was able to gain some control of his problem. When worry struck, he would know why it was happening. The next thing to understand was how to manage it, using his knowledge of his basic fear, so it would not be so controlling. He had to "own" his fear.

In a later session Hartley once again reconnected with the insecurity of his life circumstances. He got as close to the genuine feeling of fear as he could get. It was an authentic moment. He was raw. He trusted me. His eyes were wet. He sat looking at me quietly.

"Hartley, this fear, this emptiness, is part of who you are," I said. "It is not something to be disposed of. It is something to be welcomed into your family of personality parts. It is a part of you and it would be good to embrace that part. The effort to put that part somewhere else, to maybe even get rid of it, is only making it cry more loudly to be heard. You must instead nurture this part of you. Put your arm around this hurt, fearful little boy and assure him you will handle life's challenges and that it's not his job."

It helped Hartley see his worry as a distinct part of his personality. When he was hurt as a boy, some part of his personality was hived away from the core personality and left on its own as a little boy. He didn't mature along with the other parts of Hartley. He became a closet-ridden, fearful part of his being. He would speak up whenever Hartley was in trouble, ever so innocently doing his job. He was always craving to be heard. Frankly, he still wanted his mommy to give him unconditional love.

Of course, this description is a model of what is really going on. There is no little boy inside Hartley in any physical sense. But Hartley's recognition of the little boy as separate from his grown sense of self became the key to solving his chronic worrying. It helped him separate the worry from who he is. Whenever Hartley became worried, he "became" the worry. It engulfed him. Now he was benefiting from realizing that he may *have* worry, but he was not the worry itself.

Hartley needed a tool that replicated the experience of being told by an outside source what was going on in his head. I asked him to write himself a note that he could access easily in the future. This is what he typed and carried around with him on a handheld computer for easy reference:

> There it is; I am feeling it now. I must embrace, own this fear. I have a
> part of me that thinks his world is falling apart when certain signals are
> perceived. I must feel that little boy's feelings. I must see the link be-
> tween his fear that his mother is leaving him, that he feels his world is
> falling apart, that he feels empty and unloved—and the present feeling
> of fear. By drawing that link, by feeling it, and then by saying, "I have
> these feelings, they are part of who I am, they directly link to my angst,
> too"—then the angst will wane.

Hartley reported that reading this when he was fretful had an imme-diate, alleviating effect. When he combined this with some of the practical tools outlined in the previous section, he considered he had accomplished the mission of coming to terms with his worry.

Enhancing Self-Esteem

When your self-esteem is high you will have an easier time managing worry. Also, coming to grips with the fear underlying your worry actually serves to raise your self-esteem. As you learn to accept your fear, you also tend to feel better about yourself, which of course is what self-esteem is all about. But there are other ways to elevate your self-esteem. They are direct and, in one sense, simple. However, nothing comes for free. While these techniques are simple to describe, they are, by their very nature, challenging to implement.

Picture yourself getting into your car to drive somewhere a few miles from where you are now. Of course, you know that as you drive along you will have to deal with a variety of matters. A cyclist may swerve in front of you in order to avoid a manhole cover. A jaywalker may force you to slow down. The car right in front of you might jam on its brakes. No worries. You probably take for granted that you will have to deal with these things. Some of them may even be life threatening, but you have faith in yourself. You know you can handle whatever comes up.

That faith is key. When it comes to the thing that triggers your worry, you lack that faith. Why? We will see that it is because that trigger reminds you of a personal fear, and your self-esteem, based on an abiding faith in yourself, is not high enough to compensate.

Consider Joyce, a client I saw for a period of twelve weeks. She was a home-care nurse. When we spent time together she had sixteen patients spread across town. Joyce spent her days going from one patient's house to another. She tended to work alone, visiting each patient, checking in on current health matters, entering data into a portable computer, and moving on. She liked her job. It gave her lots of freedom.

One worry bout of many she described for me was particularly frightening for her. She explained that she was waiting for her husband at the family cottage. It was a Friday night and traffic was bad on the way to "cottage country." He was supposed to be there by 6:00 P.M. Joyce had come up the day before, in order to avoid the traffic. By 9:00 P.M. Joyce was in panic mode. Her husband had not arrived and had not called her from the road. He had a mobile phone and usually was pretty good about staying in touch.

Joyce and I talked about the possibility of having faith during worrisome times in order to alleviate the anxiety. We talked about how some people use their faith in God as a source of strength. Other people, we said, have faith in themselves—faith that they will effectively deal with whatever comes up, similar to our belief in ourselves when we drive down a busy roadway.

I asked Joyce what she lost faith in to make her so anxious while waiting for her husband. "Was it a matter of not having faith in your husband?"

"No, Wally's a good driver and I trust him to do what he says he'll do."

"What was it, then?"

Joyce paused, calmly running through the possibilities.

"Let's see. Well, I was afraid he was in an accident. I was afraid he was hurt. I visualized how stressed he would be if there was a crash. I knew how afraid he would be. I was afraid he was killed in an accident."

Joyce started to cry. Her thoughts were taking her to her deeper fears. "I feel so guilty," she said.

"Why guilty, Joyce?"

"Because my fears were selfish."

"How so?"

"Because if he died, I would be alone! It's so terrible of me. I think I was more worried about being left alone than I was about him!"

"And what would it mean to be alone?"

Then the tears came in a flood. "I don't want to be alone! I would be so empty! I feel so empty! And I feel so guilty for saying this! I'm so sorry, Wally!"

I got her to set the guilt aside for a moment and stay with her fear of being alone. I asked her, "Where does that fear come from, Joyce? Why are you so afraid of being alone?"

She answered that the fear of being alone was her most frightening thought. She had grown so accustomed to letting Wally manage their affairs that she could not envision surviving without him.

I repeated the big question: "So, if we go back to how worried you were and we link it to a lack of faith in something—what did you lack faith in?"

"Myself. I lacked faith that I could deal with being alone. I was frightened of being all by myself. I have no faith in myself."

Faith in oneself is the touchstone of self-esteem. One of the characteristics of people with high self-esteem is their firm belief that they will be able to deal with whatever life delivers. So Joyce and I turned to the topic of self-esteem.

Can self-esteem be manufactured? We have already referred to how knowing oneself and one's fear more intimately tends to allow self-esteem to blossom, but can we just produce it? This is a huge question.

My experience is that the challenge of elevating self-esteem is best met indirectly. The most powerful tool is to start doing things you don't want to do. It seems strange, but it's true.

Joyce took the subway to reach my office for her visit one day and I presumed she was going to take the subway on her return trip. I said to her, with a smile, "Tell me, when you get off the subway and you walk along the platform to the exit, what existential choice do you face?"

She didn't know what I was getting at.

"Well," I said, "do you take the stairs or the escalator in order to get to ground level?"

"I take the escalator. Why do you ask?"

Not wanting to overburden her, I asked her if it was a long escalator ride. When she said it was not too bad, I said, "Good—take the stairs."

"What?"

"Take the stairs."

"Okay, but why?"

"Because you don't want to."

"What does this have to do with my worry problem?"

"Everything. It is time you practiced the art of overriding your impulses. I'm not kidding."

Joyce scrunched her nose and tilted her head as if to ask, "Are you crazy?"

I explained this simple principle that I learned, albeit in a different context, from the writings of M. Scott Peck. When we feel worry, there is an impulse inside us that we give in to. What a worrier has to learn is how not to give in to it. We have to practice the skill of overriding these body impulses. The ability to override impulses is one manifestation of self-esteem.

I asked Joyce to try it for the fourteen days between our visits. Three times a day she had to do things she didn't like doing. If she wanted ice cream, she had to wait fifteen minutes. If she wanted to go home quickly, she had to take the long route instead. They had to be little things for the prescription to be realistic.

There are some very interesting reasons why overriding impulses works. The most interesting one to me is based on the principle that self-esteem goes down when we give in to our physical and social impulses. Giving in is like insulting the self.

This was terrible news for Joyce. It's bad news for many people. After all, if you'll forgive the circularity, most of us like what we like and don't like what we don't like. Joyce's plea was, "Are you telling me I have to go on a diet?" I hadn't actually thought of that possibility, but I couldn't help but respond as a traditional therapist: "Do you think you should go on a diet?"

Ultimately, Joyce and I settled on the initially stated challenge. Three times a day, for fourteen days, she would do little things she didn't want to do.

Two weeks later she returned with a smile on her face. "I actually feel better!" she said. "Every time I took the stairs, by the time I got to the top, I looked back and said, just like in the movies, 'I did that.' I worried a bit over the last two weeks, but not as much as usual. And I do honestly feel better about myself."

Over time, Joyce did get adequate control over her bouts of worry. A combination of following the practical guidelines, getting connected with her root fears, and elevating her self-esteem did the job. When circumstances arose that historically would have evoked a severe worry response, she was better able to preempt a severe reaction. She felt more in control because she knew she could control her impulses. She knew where they came from and she accepted them as helpful parts of her personality.

It takes courage to deal with a worry problem. It can be likened to descending a dark stairwell to the basement of a haunted house in search of a spooky clanging sound. We fear what we might find. But getting down there, finding the light switch, exploring the place, we discover what we knew all along. There is a source for every noise. There are no ghosts. Next time, we'll have faith in ourselves.

If You Work with a Worrier

There are two aspects to people's worries: the thing they are worried about and the tendency to worry. It's fine to help somebody address a particular worry occasion, but later it might be good to raise the topic of the tendency itself.

If it's the object of the worry you're going to help with, get a sense for whether things appear to be under control. Sometimes worriers go into paralysis and don't have any thoughts about what must be done. Is there a clear goal? Is there a plan to achieve the goal? Are there response plans to the things that could go wrong? You can help with these things.

Here's a twofold guideline for you: (1) let the worrier speak, and (2) hear the worrier. Don't say, "Don't worry about it"—that can be very invalidating. Instead, try to get to the nub of the worry: "What are you worried about?" followed by "And what if that happened?" Usually the latter question will have to be posed a few times before you get close to the bottom of the fear. Then you need to express understanding of that fear.

For example, consider somebody who is afraid that a sale they have been pitching will be lost. They might initially say that they are afraid it will affect their performance against quota. With more questions, they might get to, "But if this keeps going, I could lose my job and then I'd be out of work and I might not be able to get more work and I might not be able to provide for my family." Notice the movement from a single sale lost to utter desolation (starving kids, etc.). Getting to the root fear can do the trick. It can be relieving just to say it out loud.

Then there is a choice you can offer: The worrier can either sit back and let all those terrible things happen, or stand up and deal with them in whatever way they can be sorted out. Action plans—to reach goals or overcome possible problems—are key.

Help the worrier to see that although it's logically possible for all of these things to happen, a lot of terrible things must fall into place for such an outcome. Then they are ready for a pep talk of sorts, such as "I know you better than that" or "You will succeed." Offer whatever supportive reminders you can about how you have seen them handle problems successfully in the past.

And, most important, get them moving. Even if they are worrying about something completely out of their control, about which there is simply no room for action planning, diversion can be relieving. They need to get busy, preferably doing something of value.

The biggest value you can bring to a worrier is self-awareness. At a time when a particular threat has subsided, tell the worrier that you can see a pattern. You feel bad that there is this pattern. Wouldn't it be great if they could place their worry in a larger context the next time it arises? Wouldn't it be great if they could say, "Ah, this is the type of thing that typically pushes my buttons. But I know from experience that once my buttons are pushed, I descend into a pattern of fretting unnecessarily. Having seen this so much in myself, this time, I'm going to transcend this pattern. I'll make plans to address possibilities and I'll get busy with my goals. My mental health is reflected by how I manage my emotions, not by the fact that I have them."

CHAPTER 2

The Controller

Have you ever called someone a "control freak"? Has anyone ever called you one? For some of us the desire to control is an intermittent behavior pattern. For others, it's what defines us. Certainly our workplaces and homes have their fair share of this personality type.

Being a controlling type of person is not necessarily a bad thing. Controllers, if they know what they are doing, tend to get good things done. As a matter of fact, the tendency to control is often what gets a person promoted into positions of greater authority. Controllers tend to be deliberate and assertive in their approach, which often is recognized as bringing value to an organization.

But there are several downsides to the controller's behavior. Controllers face significant stress when they can't actually get the control they seek. For example, they may be surrounded by people who, at least in their perception, can't do what must be done. Or, they may have so much going on that they can't quite get control. Just watch controllers when their company is reorganized or changes hands. They need control, can't get it, and suddenly find themselves stymied. Frustrated controllers can get pretty wound up. Conflict, either out in the open, behind closed doors, or inside their hearts and minds, is the inevitable result.

In this chapter we look at how controllers behave, what problems they create, what's behind the urge to control, and how they can get control of control.

How Controllers Behave

Controllers assert themselves, sometimes very intensely. Both consciously and unconsciously they bear down on the world around them to satisfy their wants.

One of my clients, Rick, sought help for both the self-imposed stress caused by his tendency and the complaints he received from coworkers. Rick is a senior executive in a telecommunications company. People around him were complaining that he was "pushy" and "intense." He believed that rumors were spreading about how tough he was to work for, and he was afraid that his career might be hurt by these rumors.

For the life of him, Rick couldn't see what the fuss was all about. He was certain that his controlling style got him to his current position. He did recall, though, that a senior HR leader had told him recently that the higher up he went in the organization, the more he would have to contain himself and develop a more graceful communication style. Maybe there was some wisdom to that advice.

Rick has piercing eye contact. He is highly intelligent. He wastes no words on niceties, clearly preferring to stay focused on the task at hand. When you speak to him or, more precisely, when he speaks to you, there is no feeling of empathy coming back at you. There is just mission and strategy.

In order to determine the extent of his problem, I asked him whether it was okay for me to talk with some of his direct reports. Rick had no problem with the request. After all, that would be a direct route to the challenge at hand. The staff I interviewed consistently claimed that Rick was the quintessential controller. Two people alluded to what had become company lore: that when Rick becomes frustrated because he is not getting what he wants, he "snorts and puffs like an angry, wild animal." There was no doubt in my mind that Rick's career was at risk of being harmed by his image.

Knowing that there was no disagreement between Rick and me about his being a very dominant, controlling personality, I asked him the obvious question: "Why do you behave this way?"

Without missing a beat, Rick replied, "It's who I am. I tend to be faster and smarter than those around me. I see nuance. I know what needs to be done. I know where I'm taking things. If people just did it my way—and I know that sounds arrogant—we would save a lot of time and achieve more of our goals. It's who I am."

I accepted that. The next question was, "Is it working for you?"

"Well, not right now."

"Why?"

"Our CEO has indicated that the feedback he is getting from my peers and apparently from human resources is that I am too aggressive for my own good. I have expressed interest in the role of chief operating officer of the parent company, and this issue could hold me back. I want to address it in order to remove the obstacle."

"If your style is not serving you favorably, why do you persist in exhibiting it?" I asked.

Rick gave the typical answer offered by controllers. "I don't know how to control it," he said. "On a good day, I'm fine. But when things aren't right, okay, it just comes from inside. I can't help it."

"How do you feel when it just starts coming out?"

"Angry," he replied. "I get intense. When somebody doesn't get it, okay, I can feel my blood pressure rise."

The "okays" he kept inserting into his sentences were part of his communication style. Intense controllers sometimes use such tools to control the thoughts of the other person. It's as if they're saying, "First I want you to think this particular thought. Okay, now that you have had that thought, I want you to have this thought. Don't have other thoughts! Just think what I tell you to think."

So anger was one topic Rick and I addressed. We had to explore why not getting what he wanted made him so angry. Through multiple sessions we traced it to pain he had experienced in his childhood. He wanted more of his father's attention than he was getting. This pain was never really processed. It was unresolved. Rick learned both to avoid the pain and to satisfy his needs. His tool was to impress his father. He learned to be a take-charge man, just like his father was. But all along Rick has feared this pain. When his efforts to eradicate and avoid the pain looked like they were going to fail, he would get angry.

Notice that his fear was not expressed as worry. This was not his particular response to the possibility of revisiting his pain. Instead, Rick learned over his lifetime to leverage his strong will in response to his fear. He became controlling. To reduce his controlling orientation, he had to confront his fear and process his unresolved pain.

Rick's deputies described him as a poor delegator. They explained that he only partly communicated what must be done and then would get involved when people weren't doing what he wanted. This, too, is a common problem for people with controlling personalities. Sometimes they undercommunicate in order to justify getting back involved. Sometimes they are simply poor communicators who assign projects ineffectively. Sometimes they unfairly judge people as incapable and think "this person is going to screw up anyway so I'll just get them started and step in a little later." Often they simply underestimate the amount of control they want to have over how something gets done. This was the case with Rick. He just wanted complete control over everything.

It's not that Rick was a perfectionist; he wanted things done his way, but it was easy for him to allow his staff to make mistakes and ignore correcting them. He just tended to control. If perfectionism had been another trait on top of his controlling orientation, he would have been even tougher to work for. People might feel that on top of working for someone who did not empower them, they were running around after trivialities.

Suzanne is a good example of a controlling perfectionist. A vice president of marketing for a midsize furniture-manufacturing company, she drove people in her office crazy by catching them on the smallest wayward detail and landing on them for it. Unlike Rick, who tended to control areas linked to his various short-term and long-term goals, Suzanne controlled whatever affected her image.

For Suzanne, gaining the esteem of others at all costs called for a perfectionistic approach to everything she touched. She cared very much about how she was perceived by others. It showed up in how she maintained her house (expensively designed and furnished, always tidy), her car (expensive, always clean, inside and out), her clothes (always current and very expensive), her hair and her makeup, her office, her stationery, her choice of assistant ("a master's degree in romantic literature, don't you know"), her on-the-job style. When Suzanne had the slightest opportunity to impress, she took it.

I first met Suzanne while I was attending a board meeting to observe someone else I was coaching. Before the meeting began, I overheard her chatting with a new colleague. In less than five sentences, she managed to communicate that her daughter was a national gymnastics contestant but didn't make the top three; this same daughter was going to the most prestigious medical school in the country but it had been a real struggle to get in; her husband was negotiating for a private jet (wow, are they ever expensive); her son may have graduated first in his class in his freshman year of engineering, but "gosh, did he have to work hard. It's not fair how they make them work."

Suzanne was reasonably skilled at looking humble while carefully demonstrating that she was special. Image was her driving force. She was controlling because she had to sustain that image. I remember thinking how challenging she would be to coach. I got my chance to find out: A month later she called for help.

Coaching Suzanne about her controlling and perfectionistic orientation was indeed quite difficult. Like Rick, she had to wrestle with fear. All children periodically experience a craving for more love, security, and attention than they are getting at the time. When it occurs frequently enough and severely enough, however, they will build a defense of some kind to prevent recurrence. A fear drives the creation and maintenance of that defense system.

However, that fear manifested itself differently in Suzanne's case than in Rick's. Rick's response to deep pain and insecurity was to do what his father did and liked to see in his boy: Take charge, keep control. His style in doing so was characterized as pushy, intense, task oriented, and sometimes angry. Suzanne's response to deep insecurity was to fill in its corollary emptiness with the respect and affection of others by being perfect and behaving perfectly. Achieving perfection for Suzanne could only be fully achieved through complete control.

Rick and Suzanne had two different styles of response to the core fears that settled in as they experienced life, but their responses led them both to develop problematic controlling personalities. Other controllers develop differently. For example, some prideful people cannot relinquish control of their position in an argument even in the face of obvious contrary evidence. They come across as controlling because they just won't let up. The aversion to being wrong locks them up. Their obstinacy is their control. If they lose their control, they think they are worthless.

Many controllers are tricky. They use a variety of techniques to control others. They don't come across as controllers, initially, but their techniques are effective, just the same. Some examples:

■ I remember a client who only made love with her husband when she wanted something important from him. And he never knew the difference.

■ Another client avoided all significant effort and, controlling every detail from afar, delegated to her assistant and her husband everything she wanted done. It wasn't that she was lazy. Her fear was that if she had to do the work herself, she would soon be found out to be a failure.

■ Another client used guilt as his primary tool to control the people close to him. He positioned himself as a victim and found subtle ways to make it clear that if people loved him, they would help him out—in ways he would happily describe for them. He was fearful that if he couldn't get people to serve him, then he would be of no significance in the world.

■ Still another client always positioned himself as knowing more than everyone else. He controlled people's views of him by what he didn't say specifically but only alluded to. He was afraid he would not be successful unless he had the respect of others.

There are also many controllers who don't get into trouble over it. As a matter of fact, most of us are controllers to some extent, depending on the people we are dealing with and the circumstances involved. People influence others consciously and unconsciously all the time. Many long-term marriages go through stages of struggling for control and relinquishing control. There is also a natural control dynamic in most employee-employer relationships. The primary reason to address control is when it is a cause of problems.

The Problems Controllers Create

Controllers get themselves into trouble. Both Rick and Suzanne had been complained about. Their coworkers felt mistrusted. Working for someone like Rick, who does not delegate well and who tends to step in to take away your control over your project, means feeling that you're being judged "not good enough." Working for a perfectionist like Suzanne means being told that what you did was not good enough. Funny thing— people don't like being treated in these ways.

Often controllers create fear in the minds of their employees. Rick, for example, would raise his voice, "breathe funny," and generally make people feel that somehow problems on the job were going to become physical in some way. He would tremble in anger and others would tremble in fear.

Some bosses motivate their workers by inspiring them to think independently and encouraging them to fulfill themselves on the job. Controllers don't usually create this type of environment. People who work for them often end up being motivated by fear. Their employees feel depleted or smaller in some way when they are being robbed of their freedom to do things their way.

Employees of highly controlling leaders often harbor great resentment over their bosses. It's an automatic response. Controlled people feel invalidated. This tends to deplete their self-esteem—their beliefs that they have value and are able. When self-esteem declines, so, too, do things like the ability to learn, think creatively, and participate optimally on a team. Motivation goes down. Productivity goes down. Morale goes down. No wonder controllers seek help!

Of course, all this declining momentum around effectiveness creates a self-fulfilling prophecy for the controller. People don't do things well when they feel this way. This motivates the controller to step in and, in the long run, make things worse.

Another big problem controllers cause is the stifling of creativity. For example, they are abysmal at running brainstorming sessions. It's not just that their style makes people less likely to open up and contribute their ideas. It's that their style shuts down discussion altogether. There is simply no contribution from other people. Disagreement is what sometimes creates new ideas. When controllers disallow disagreement, they stop the momentum of creative thinking.

Many controllers regret that people around them are hurting. Rick, for example, reported that he always felt remorse after losing his temper. Suzanne felt bad that she was disliked by her coworkers and, sometimes, even by her husband. Ironically, this disliking of her behavior was the very opposite of the affection the behavior was intended to generate.

What's Behind Controlling?

Everyone is somewhere on the continuum of controlling. A handy way to see this is to consider psychologist Robert Ornstein's theory of deliberate versus liberate thinking styles. Controlling types tend to be more "deliberate," while, on the other side of the midpoint on the scale, more relaxed, spontaneous people are "liberate."

You can see the extreme deliberate style in somebody who is compulsive about something. For example, a former client of mine is compulsive about washing his hands. After he touches almost anything outside of his home, he wants to wash his hands before he touches anything else. A little less extreme, but still on the deliberate side of the continuum, is someone who tends to be fairly regimented in her approach to things. This person likes things done in a certain way. A little closer to the middle, but still deliberate in style, is someone who simply likes to keep things organized or structured.

Three similar degrees of the liberate type could be described like this: Someone we might call "flaky" (unpredictable and unreliable) would be at the extreme end, someone we might call "creative" not as far over, and someone who is simply "interesting" closer to the middle. The flaky person is the total opposite of someone compulsive, who is the extreme deliberate type.

The controlling personality would fit on the deliberate side, probably somewhere well away from the middle. Controllers don't just like structure; they like regimentation, predictability, and compliance.

Let's explore the act of controlling to get a better understanding of what's behind it. People control because they want something to happen. They are afraid that without their control, that thing won't happen. The question is, what's wrong with that? Why the fear?

I hear various answers to that question during coaching sessions. Some people say they don't want to lose what is theirs. Others say they might not be liked anymore. Many simply report that they won't be okay if they don't get what they want. That probably points to the heart of the matter. People associate control with being okay or safe. For all controllers, there is discomfort around not getting what they want. Behind the act of controlling hides an unresolved feeling of not being okay and a fear of revisiting that feeling.

Many controllers will tell you that the thing they want control over simply needs to be controlled, given some goal. They will say theirs is the most efficient and effective means to the goal. "If you don't follow the instructions, the recipe won't turn out." But this defense rarely accounts for the motivation behind their controlling behavior. For conversations about control to be effective, they must point to a problematic pattern rather than an idiosyncratic event.

My experience is that there is always a pain behind the tendency to control excessively. The fear of not being okay does not arise out of the blue. Sometime in each controller's life there was a threat to being okay and the response to that threat was fear. A recurrence of that threat evokes the same response.

It probably was not a single occasion that put a controller's well-being in jeopardy. It was more likely a recurring scenario. Suzanne, the image-conscious woman, had a sister who always got more attention than she did. Her sister was thought to be better looking. Suzanne hated the feeling of being loved less. She compensated by working harder to gain people's respect and validation. She became a controller of situations, such that she would always make things the way she thought would opti-mize the chance of validation from others. Controlling her image helped her cope, not only with her unresolved pain but also with situations that might make her revisit that pain.

Rick, the man who huffed and puffed when things weren't going his way, traced his fear back to years of watching his father manage a small business. His father gave Rick affection when Rick behaved deliberately. This conditional love offering caused him pain. But he learned to satisfy the condition. His father positively reinforced Rick's style of getting things done. When Rick had things under control, Rick was treated with respect. That's how he learned to earn his father's validation. "Be the one dominating, not the victim of someone else's domination or of a team's inadequacy," was the message. He feared that he wouldn't be loved if he didn't control.

Notice that Rick and Suzanne used control to get what they needed: Rick needed to behave in a certain way in order to feel worthy, while

Suzanne needed to gain the respect of others. But consider this very different but very common dynamic in controllers: Some people control not to get closer to what they seek, but to move away from, or block, what they don't want. In this scenario, fear still plays a key role.

Take Jim, for example. He is a medical doctor considered by his family, friends, patients, and coworkers to be a very controlling man. It's easy for a busy family practitioner to adopt a controlling style. Medicine demands compliance with established protocols, and medical doctors are placed on a social pedestal: a perfect context for domination and control. But in Jim's case, it was something different.

In several dialogues with me in my office, Jim revealed that he controls in order to block other things from getting in. Unlike Rick, who controls to get closer to his fulfillment, Jim controls to move away from his demons. He feels that if he lightens up, then, as he put it, "Who knows what would happen!" Let's see how Jim learned how to get excessive controlling "under control."

Getting Control of Control

Jim's clinic at the hospital had arranged an off-site meeting where they would review their performance over the last year, address some administrative issues in the department, open up lines of communication, and develop their sense of team. Prior to the four-day meeting, the HR department of the hospital had initiated a "360-degree review" process, in which people were given a chance to provide feedback on each of their coworkers. The idea was to collect all the feedback prior to the meeting and make it available during the meeting itself. At the meeting, people were given a chance to speak one-on-one with colleagues to get clarity on the comments about them.

This was a great first step in Jim's evolution away from being a highly controlling person. I've seen this work several times. By giving the people around the controller the chance to say what is on their minds, the controller becomes more aware of the consequences of his style. Jim learned that although his colleagues and some of his patients respected his technical skills, they found his bedside manner laughable. Further, he found out that nurses and technicians dreaded talking to him because they knew their opinion would never be welcome and Jim would talk down to them as though they were children and incompetent.

Jim was saddened by the feedback he received. He had always known he was dominating but was unaware of its impact. When he went home, he told his wife what he had learned about himself at the meeting. She supported him during his sadness but also filled in the picture from her angle. She lovingly communicated that even though she was accustomed to letting him be in charge, she sometimes resented it. At one point she told him that not only was he controlling, but he was compulsive about some things as well.

"For heaven's sake, Jim," she said, "we're the only family I know that washes out plastic bags and turns them inside out to dry so that we can use them again! You need help, Jim!"

Jim had all sorts of professional resources available to him. But he wanted to "manage the optics." He and I had met at school and stayed in touch over the years. He called me for help. Our work together focused on two distinct matters: his communication style and his controlling orientation. We dealt with communication matters first because regardless of why Jim controlled people, he could certainly start changing right away by interacting with them differently.

Controllers often are highly task-oriented people who lose sight of the humanity around them. By staying too focused on task, they miss the human needs. For controlling personalities to be less caustic in their relationships, they have to find ways to incorporate empathy into their communication.

Empathy means feeling what others feel. It is different from sympathy, the recognition of how others feel. For example, if I told you that Larry, my pet goldfish, passed away, quietly, in his bowl, you might look me in the eye, shake my hand, and say, "Sorry about the fish." Sympathy is like that. The sympathetic person gets to stay on the sidelines paying respect and feeling bad for the victim. Empathy, however, involves actually taking on the feelings of the other party. If I were lamenting the loss of my fish, and you were empathetic toward me, you would join me in my grief.

By incorporating genuine empathy into your style—not sympathy, which allows you to stay on the sidelines—you will undoubtedly project less of a controlling image. When people feel the connection created by the expression of empathy, they feel validated, the opposite of what they feel when they are being controlled. The challenge in using empathy is in accessing it.

I believe that most people are born with the capacity for empathy. It is hardwired right into the nervous system because it is a key part of species survival. Parents are better parents when they are compassionate, and societal bonding calls for some degree of interpersonal commonality at an emotional level.

The initial off-site meeting that Jim attended set the stage for his learning about empathy. He began at that meeting to understand how people felt about him. He realized that their observations of his style were not just intellectual; they were emotional. Jim felt bad about hurting people's feelings, and he also began to feel empathy for the people he had hurt.

Next, Jim had to learn how to incorporate empathy into his day-to-day communication. He had to learn to take a few moments in most dialogues to ask himself how the other person was probably feeling about the dialogue, and he had to learn to address those likely feelings either directly or indirectly. For example, rather than saying to a patient who had been prescribed a complex regimen of pills, "Have you been staying on the meds like I said?" Jim learned to say, "I know that was quite a complex bunch of instructions to follow; how has it been going?"

Jim had no problem adopting this approach in much of his professional communication. He was a very motivated learner. He couldn't accept being a man in a healing profession who was doing psychological damage, even in some small way.

Jim told me his biggest challenge was speaking empathetically to people he didn't like. Some of the technicians and other doctors were not, in his eyes, worthy of much respect. As he put it, "I really don't care how those guys feel. Am I supposed to fake it with them or just stay on task?" He did not want to fake it and he did not want to drop the ball in one area while making progress in other areas. He wanted to do this right. So we spent time locating authentic compassion for the people he didn't like. We did it by analyzing them together and discovering how even their provocative behavior, the things that Jim did not respect in them, came from an innocent array of private hurts. Jim learned, for example, that even though he didn't respect a doctor whom he considered to be motivated by greed more than by medicine, that doctor had his own set of fears that explained his behavior.

Over time, Jim developed the skill of infusing authentic empathy into his communication. His bedside manner improved and his coworkers began to see a change in his style on the job. One day, he came for his session, updated me on his progress, and then said, "But I'm still washing out plastic bags." We laughed and got down to work on his controlling orientation.

The hardest part of Jim's progress was the time we spent focusing on why he was so "tight." He liked that word because it had two connotations that he thought could be collapsed into one appropriate descriptor. His wife called Jim "tight," referring to his being miserly (e.g., washing disposable bags to save money). Jim called himself "tight" because that was how he felt while he was at his most controlling. For him, both uses of the word meant the same thing. They referred to self-protection, an effort to keep things out.

I asked him, "What specifically are you so afraid of?"

"Well," he said, "surely it's understandable that I would have some fear of what might go wrong. I mean, I'm making hundreds of decisions a day that have a huge impact on people's lives."

I told Jim I wanted to connect with his fear rather than hearing him describe how logical it was to have a fear response.

"What do you mean?" he asked.

"Well, let's talk about the plastic bags again. Why do you wash them out?"

"Because throwing them away when they in fact could be used again is unnecessarily harmful to the environment."

"But what feeling is behind it?"

"I don't know."

I asked him to close his eyes. I knew that he would connect with the feelings driving his tendency to control if he could visualize a provocative situation. "Picture yourself in the kitchen of your home. You are doing the dishes. A piece of chicken you had for lunch was taken out of its plastic bag and the plastic bag is just lying there. Can you picture that?"

"Sure," he said, "let's go with it."

"Okay, you are walking over to it. Jim, I want you to throw out the bag. Pick it up and put it in the garbage."

"No. It's bad for the environment. It'll sit in a dump."

"Jim, on this special occasion, throw out the bag."

He chuckled and winced at the same time.

"There it is," he said. "Simple as that. There's the tightness."

I asked him to focus on the tightness and tell me what it felt like.

"It's tight in my chest."

"Good," I said. "Now can you bring a picture to mind of where that tightness is coming from?"

"It's a small mass inside my chest, like a lump of coal. It's very tight."

"If you could give it a voice, what would it say?"

"Well, first of all, this is the tightness that accompanies me on all my days. It's always there."

"Good. Tell me more."

"It's got to be like this. There can't be any other way. I have to keep them out. They just have to do what I say."

Following his lead but not knowing what he was talking about, I said, "Good, Jim. What happens if they get in, if they meddle?"

"It all comes apart."

I had to ask, even though this was the difficult moment, "What happens then, Jim?"

He paused. "Funny. A memory just popped into my head."

I urged him to go with it.

"It's a sandbox memory. I remember actually being in a sandbox in my backyard. I was fighting. I can picture myself saying, 'It's mine! It's my sandbox!'"

"What if they get in, Jim?"

"They will take it away!"

Jim's eyes opened wide and there were a few seconds of silence while he processed the connections he had just made.

Since these things are all unique to the person experiencing them— only the principle of fear being involved is universal—I was curious to hear his explanation.

He said that he was the oldest of five kids in his family. He had spent years experiencing a phenomenon time and time again. When he was young, his favorite things were given to his siblings: his clothing, his toys, time with his parents. By his midteens he was sick of it. Out of anger, he adopted the position that he would take it no longer.

"I became selfish with my time, my ideas, my principles. Nobody was going to get in."

All of Jim's controlling behavior could be explained by this model of his. On the job, he blocked people's questions because he was afraid that they would open up other possibilities and take away his ability to make things work his way. He managed family vacations because otherwise he wouldn't have a good time. He was controlling with the nurses and technicians around him—if they did not do things to the letter of his law, he might not be loved for doing things so well.

Of course, the irony was that Jim's strategy actually worked against him. After all, by including other people's opinions, the controller is more likely to reach a better conclusion about matters. But being in the rut of being a controller works that way. Controllers may reap the benefits of control, but they miss the harvest of dialogue with others.

For a controller to understand why he controls does not itself remove his long-term, deeply ingrained habit of controlling. But it can set the stage for progress. When a controller knows why he does what he does, he can begin to make different choices throughout the moments of each day. Controllers must experiment with relinquishing control and experience the fact that not having control in those instances does not represent failure or harm.

Disposing of single-use plastic bags no doubt hurt the environment. But doing so did allow Jim to experiment with letting go of control. In fact, we talked about how his desire to hold onto plastic bags was the perfect metaphor for his problem. Clear plastic bags are enclosures. You can see in them, but they are sealed. Jim liked them not so much because they didn't spoil other things in the refrigerator, but because they would protect what was in them from other things. For Jim, tightly sealed containers that kept things out were good things to retain. Our mission was to let them go. It wasn't easy for Jim, but he learned to do it, and survive.

Putting everything together, then, if you are a controller you can benefit from taking these four steps:

1. Get feedback from the people being controlled concerning the impact you have on their feelings and their subsequent efforts. This feedback will help you to learn that you are not in a vacuum. From an empathetic place, you can learn that control not only shuts people down and denies access to the value they can add; it is also hurtful.

2. Make an effort to change your basic behavior. This usually involves learning how to communicate more empathetically. A coach or mentor can give you specific instructions about how to delegate tasks and empower others.

3. Learn to detect the role of emotions in your propensity to control. This is the critical step. This explains why it is happening. People like Rick or Suzanne control to move toward something (such as love or attention) and a fear of not getting it propels them. People like Jim control to move away from something that they are afraid of (such as pain). The pain or fear of loss that plays a role in all these cases must be owned, in the sense that you ultimately must say something like, "Yes, I have this fear driving me. I accept this fear as part of who I am."

4. Recognize that along with control goes the illusion that it is necessary. When you control, you adopt a very narrow view that you happen to think is the best possible view. This is almost always an incorrect assessment. My experience is that there is always a bigger perspective that carries with it another dimension of considerations.

As a coach I sometimes touch base with the original complainants several months into a change effort to see whether change has occurred. When the controller knows that this will happen, a sense of accountability is instilled.

In following up with Rick, Suzanne, and Jim, I uncovered consistent results. All three continued to experience the impulse to control. And all three did indeed periodically fall into their old habits. But they all self-reported a reduction in their controlling tendencies. And all of them had received feedback from those around them that they were, as Jim's wife said, "not as bad."

Another consistent report pertained to the most powerful aspect of any effective effort to become less controlling. "Owning the fear" has a huge impact on success. It means the controller not only has to acknowledge that there is a fear behind keeping control, she also has to experiment with not taking control, feeling the anxiety it provokes and accepting that anxiety for what it is. One cannot hide from that anxiety—in a way, hiding from it is the source of the problem. Instead, one must stay with it for a while. Hold onto it. Realize that it is a natural but usually unwarranted defense motivated by a sincere desire to avoid angst from the past. Resting in that fear can be both invigorating and freeing.

If You Work with a Controller

If you have to survive working for or around a controller, let the controller know how it makes you feel. Also, you've got to get the controller to trust you. Increase communication substantially. Manage expectations. Avoid their disappointment by keeping them fully informed. Give them choices. Get them to be much more specific when they delegate tasks. You have to learn to "manage up," as in convincing a controller that when it comes to you, they can loosen the reins a bit. This will be enhanced if you tell the controller your aim is to please at all times.

If you are seeking to help someone be less controlling, it may take several conversations. Get them to admit that they would like to control less. Ask for permission to point out when they are being controlling. Indicate at the right moment that apparently there is a view that control links to fear. Wonder aloud about exactly what their fear is. Get them to realize that there is a pattern in the situations in which they tend to dominate: In every case they seem to fear the same things. This will elevate their self-awareness. Try to differentiate the thing they are fearing (e.g., getting in trouble with their boss) and the fact that they have fear. It's the fear itself that needs to be "owned," not the fear of, or in this case, trouble with, the boss. Ownership is about recognizing that fearfulness is a part of their makeup.

CHAPTER 3

The Fake

One of my most interesting, and unsettling, consulting projects took place over a decade ago. It started with a phone call from the president of a small stockbrokerage. He said he had a team of thirty-five brokers, and he thought morale was bad. He wanted me to come in, figure out what was wrong, and make a recommendation.

I told him I wanted to interview half of his brokers in order to get a good feeling for the situation, following which I would write an informal report. I told him the fee and he agreed instantly. Frankly, I was surprised he agreed so quickly. We set an appointment for the first round of interviews.

When I arrived a week later at his downtown office, I met with my principal briefly, who then took me on a tour of the facility. It seemed like a normal work environment for what was essentially a telemarketing organization. Small offices lined the outside walls of the one floor complex. Each office was staffed by a broker. I thought it was interesting that everyone I could see was actually on the phone at the time of my glance—quite a coincidence.

A boardroom had been reserved for my interviews, so I got a cup of coffee and settled in for my first meeting of the day.

The first interviewee seemed kind of slick. Well, he was slick. His hair was slicked back, he wore heavy gold jewelry, and he spoke quickly. He was very focused. He said he had been in the business for several years and that his own morale was fine. He operated a snowplow in the winter and held this job in the summer. That seemed strange to me, but, well, I had never done work in the brokerage industry. I asked him about the morale of the other brokers in the firm.

"Some of them are young and can't take it," he said. Then he shrugged and added, "For me, if somebody wants to buy what I have to sell, that's their problem."

The next person was one of the troubled ones. He seemed depressed. He couldn't look me in the eye. He was quick to say he disliked his job. I asked him why he stayed in the job and he responded with a simple question: "Where else can you work five hours a day and make $350,000 a year?" That caught my attention. "What exactly do you do?" I asked. He explained that he was a "loader." Other guys built new client relationships, but when any of those clients expressed interest in larger investments, he would step in. "Why do they call it a loader?" I asked. "Well, we load them up. We step in to get the client to really open his pocketbook."

After a few more interviews it all became clear. These guys were crooks! They spent their days calling people—usually not-so-financially-smart people—and selling them penny stocks, the price of which the brokers knew would rise a bit and then plummet to about nothing. When the stock would go up, the broker would call the victim client and say, "See? I told you I would take care of you. Let me know when you're ready to make some serious money." When the client was excited, it was time for the loaders.

People would mortgage their houses for these guys. People who couldn't afford any kind of investment would risk everything. Eventually they would lose everything, because the firm had complete control over the price of the stock, and virtually every stock price would plummet. The brokers were making 20 percent of every transaction. It was, as they say, highway robbery.

By late morning, I went to my principal, explained my understanding, and told him that morale was poor at his firm because some of his people couldn't cope with what they were doing to their "clients."

"My advice is that you close your doors," I said. "And I'm sorry, but I can't participate in this."

I went home early. I had never knowingly been in the company of con artists. I felt dirty.

Some of those brokers were addicted to the income and felt absolutely bound by their addiction. And they were quintessential fakes. They were engaged in an activity that was counter to what they knew in their hearts was right.

You might be thinking, "If that's what a fake is, it obviously doesn't apply to me. I am not doing anything illegal or immoral." But hold on. As a matter of fact, wrestling with a dissonance between what we do on the outside and how we feel on the inside is one of the most common topics of conversation in my coaching practice.

Bad Faith

In a sense, we're all fakes. The French existentialist philosopher Jean-Paul Sartre refers to the lies we tell to ourselves as "bad faith." He suggests that it is pretty much a capacity built right into our way of being. He doesn't mean that we knowingly tell ourselves falsehoods. He means that people have an ability to take a position on a matter even though some other part of them does not hold that position. We can experience a profound alienation from ourselves.

Examples of bad faith abound. A man in my office is late pretty much every day. His boss sometimes complains to her peers about it. But she doesn't actually confront the tardy employee. She's committing bad faith. She knows it's not okay with her that this employee is late. She intends to act on it some day. Her lie, her fakery, is in letting it go on without addressing it.

Addictions are great examples of bad faith. Somebody knows he wants to quit smoking. He stomps out his last cigarette and declares to the universe, "That's it. I quit." And then, an hour later, some trigger prompts him to reach for another smoke. He recalls his declaration but leaps past its meaning with the thought, "I'll quit later." At that moment, he is in bad faith.

Extramarital affairs are prime examples of bad faith. At the time we are romancing our new friend, we are usually deceiving ourselves. We ignore one truth for the sake of another more appealing one.

But being a fake is not just about tricking ourselves. It's also about tricking others—not necessarily intending to trick them, but just participating in it. Let's look at some examples.

The Truth Is, I May Not Measure Up

Catherine walked around all day with a gnawing feeling that there was something wrong. She couldn't define it. She was a senior vice president of a globally recognized transportation conglomerate. Catherine was trained as an economist and was considered very knowledgeable. As a leader of a team of vice presidents, who in turn were responsible for several layers of workers numbering in the hundreds, she held a very powerful position.

Catherine's days involved speaking with government leaders and her executive colleagues and attending strategy meetings with her deputies. But something undesirable was always at the back of her mind.

Initially she came to me looking for help because of feedback she had received through her performance review. She couldn't deny what she had been told. Various important people had indicated to her boss that they were frustrated with her. When they asked her questions, she couldn't produce the answers they wanted. She talked too much in meetings. Her deputies lamented that she was unclear and meandering.

Catherine wanted practical coaching advice to overcome these behavioral challenges.

"If the feedback you have received is true, that you're not getting to the point clearly and quickly enough, what's the reason?" I asked her. After some dialogue, she expressed that possibly she was not up to the job.

"As a matter of fact," she said, "I'm frightened to death about it."

Catherine told me of dreams she had in which she was, in various ways, always looking like a fool in front of others. Her performance review made her feel that the dreams were coming true. Her eyes showing vulnerability, she asked, "Can you fix it?"

The first valuable insight for her was that the gnawing feeling of something being wrong was easily explained. It was fear. The fear was understandable. Her job called for a certain level of knowledge and skill and she felt she wasn't up to it. Her lack of confidence was anxiety provoking. Her fakery was in the difference between her outside persona— her role, her image—and her inner concept of herself.

Why did Catherine's fakery show up in her dialogues with people? Well, when asked questions about parts of the job in which she felt insecure, her brain would not let her get to the point, lest she be found out. She would go on and on, never really landing on the target point. She was so busy hiding her truth, she couldn't get to any truth. In meetings with her deputies, she feared that they would figure out that she didn't know what she was doing.

The interesting thing is that her insecurity was, in one sense, quite valid. She had a tough job in a challenging industry. When you're pioneering, you're not going to know everything. In another sense, her insecurity was quite unwarranted. She actually was capable of the job. It was her fear of not being capable that was causing the problem. It became a block to healthy communication.

Catherine's recovery came from learning to accept her limitations and coming to believe that, even with her limitations, she was acceptable. When she made headway in this direction, an amazing irony took shape. She became more respected. Imagine that! Acknowledging one's limitations leads to being held in higher esteem!

She didn't just have to acknowledge her limitations and her fears to herself; she also had to disclose them—with some finesse, of course—to others. As a matter of fact, the primary solution to her problem was in allowing herself to reveal her limitations—not her fears, but the real-life challenges she faced—to others. She learned to say things like, "Well, that *is* a monster problem" or "I actually don't have the faintest idea at this stage, but I'm sure we can sort it out."

When the secret was out, the fear of being caught with it disappeared.

I Don't Deserve the Respect I Get

Many actors, politicians, physicians, and leaders of all types get all sorts of applause and respect but deep down don't feel deserving of it.

I recall a well-known trainer and facilitator whose job was to stand in front of large audiences amusing them, teaching them things they really appreciated. His name was Daniel. At the end of his presentations, the audience would applaud. Sometimes he would even receive a standing ovation. He told me he always made a certain gesture during the applause time. He would raise his arms so all could see, and he would applaud back. He was attempting to say to the audience, "No, no . . . it's you who deserve the credit." He thought it was a humble way to deal with the incoming appreciation.

Actually, Daniel was one of those people who can never take a compliment. Tell him you liked his shirt and he would make a quick reply that somehow deflected the praise. "Yes, I like it, too—my wife has great taste." Notice in his response that Daniel wasn't letting the praise in. He didn't know how to let it in. Why? Well, his unspoken view of himself was that he was not so special. When someone said he was special, it just didn't register.

Daniel's fakery was obviously in his head. There was no dissonance between what he was doing and what he was capable of doing. After all, he was the guy doing what merited the applause. Daniel's fakery was an illusion. He had the sense that he didn't deserve the credit so he felt awkward about acknowledging it.

The solution to Daniel's problem came in learning to accept his weaknesses. One day he acknowledged, at least to me, that he wasn't good in one particular area and didn't have credentials in another area. He went on and on trying to justify his feeling of fraudulence.

"I don't really have the data to back up my claims. Sometimes people ask me questions and I have to bluff my answers. Sometimes I speak to groups and don't even know if what I'm saying applies. I often don't have the time to research my audience. Okay, okay, sometimes I wing it!"

"So, even with all those limitations, are you bringing value to those groups of people?" I asked him. His somewhat reluctant answer was in the affirmative. I pressed on. "And, tell me, do you wing well?"

"I am a good winger," he said.

I knew that relief was around the corner. "Do you forgive yourself for winging? Can you accept yourself for not having all the data to back up your claims?"

"Well, now that you mention it, I guess I don't have much choice."

Daniel was able to declare to himself, "I am just Daniel, and that's okay."

His presentations changed a bit as a result. He spent more time being honest with his audiences. For example, he would change a sentence like "People think at the rate of 450 words per minute" to "My impression is that people think very quickly, much faster than they speak."

Daniel felt better. He even learned to take a humble bow while receiving applause and then look at the audience, usually focusing on a few individuals, and mouth the words "thank you."

I Am Not of Value

A client named Roxanne complained of feeling tense, jittery, all day at work. She also felt depressed most of the time. I asked her if she thought she was good at her job. Her answer was no. "Do you bring value to your organization?" "No," was her reply.

The best way to understand Roxanne is to think of her as having a running hypothesis in her head that she was not okay. When things occurred that contradicted her hypothesis, such as someone giving her a compliment on her work, she would dismiss it. She would chalk it up to the person's not really knowing the truth about her.

But whenever she made a mistake on the job, that was a different story. To her, it was evidence that her hypothesis was valid. She would quickly think to herself, "Yup, that proves it," and then she'd become depressed.

How was Roxanne a fake? In her own mind, she was not worthy of her job. She had the job. On the surface, she behaved as though she was fine in the job. But her private view was that she was a fraud.

Not that she was aware of all of this, of course. No, like Daniel and Catherine, she just felt crummy most of the time but didn't know why.

People like she often have a self-image that holds them back. They believe, deep down, that they are really not of value. According to Nathaniel Branden, this is a sign of low self-esteem. Branden says there are two beliefs that are touchstones for healthy self-esteem: the belief that one is able, and the belief that one is worthy. Roxanne's challenge was to learn to affirm the latter belief.

The origin of a low self-image can usually be traced to childhood. When parents fail to tell kids they are able and worthy, the kids have little reason to believe in themselves. But it's not always a parenting issue. A series of problematic life experiences can cause the problem. Bosses who don't positively reinforce employees can contribute to low self-esteem.

This, of course, is a big problem, because bosses want people to have initiative and an "I can do this" attitude.

In Roxanne's case, there was the claim, "I am of low value." That made coaching her relatively easy. She just had to learn to accept her limitations and her strengths. We talked a lot about how this kind of self-acceptance, regardless of a lifetime of conditioning, can be effected through choice. When one sees one's pattern, and can rationally refute the logic behind the pattern, one is able to recognize a role for choice. Ultimately Roxanne was able to say, "I have a recurring line of thinking that proclaims my being of low value. However, rationally I know where this comes from and that it is not necessarily valid. I know that I am in my job for a reason. I will make mistakes. But I can choose my outlook. I choose to accept my history, my mistakes, and I choose to adopt an attitude of hope and faith in myself."

Sometimes it's not that easy, however. Some people say, "I know I have a poor self-image, but no matter what I do, I can't change it." And they are able to bring forth convincing evidence of their position.

I can't help but think of a man named Frank. He and I reached that place in our relationship where he declared, "My self-image is terribly poor." I responded by pointing out that there may not be any need for him to hold that position.

"After all," I said, "you are an engineer. You are a respected vice president of manufacturing in a much-respected company. You have friends and parents who love you."

Frank's answer was simple and put me on the spot.

"Look," he said, "we both know that by anybody's definition I am not very attractive. I've never had a girlfriend and I'm forty-seven years old. I have a pockmarked, unsymmetrical face, I am out of shape, and no female has ever been interested in me. Who am I trying to kid? I really am of no value."

Beyond the compassion that I'm sure I expressed, through my eyes, I didn't have an immediate answer. I couldn't dismiss his claims out of hand. I knew the mission was to get him to accept himself for what he was. I knew we could and would explore social constructs and their artificiality. But his argument was that he wanted a woman and couldn't get one. And it hurt him deeply.

Where was Frank's fakery? He spent his days with a gnawing regret over being alone. On the job, he was an impostor. He went about his day-to-day job pretending to be okay, whereas inside, he was a wreck.

We did work on self-acceptance. We did look at how the media construct social definitions for beauty. We did explore the possibility of acceptance. To keep him busy, I convinced him to be active outside of work. He joined a badminton club. That's where he eventually met his wife. Thank goodness.

Frank, like Roxanne, had access to his feelings. Both of them had a poor self-image and they knew it. But that leads us to that group of people who have a poor self-image and don't know it.

William comes to mind. He was an extraordinarily successful man who came across as dynamic, powerful, controlling, bright, and together. However, William was psychologically addicted to marijuana and he had an absolutely terrible temper.

Where was his fraudulence? He was hurting inside. And he had completely masked his pain. We uncovered that his parents, during his childhood forty-five years prior, had virtually ignored him, largely due to the fact that his sibling was severely handicapped and needed a lot of their attention.

William's problems faded away as he was able to attribute his problematic behaviors, one-by-one, to his feeling of emptiness inside. He realized that he was a dominating control freak because of his mistaken belief that if he wasn't in control, he would reexperience his childhood angst. He was a know-it-all because if he were perceived not to have answers, that, too, would take him back to his pain. His temper was volatile because his anger at being neglected was always just beneath the surface.

The Active Deceiver

One client, Tom, came to see me about problems he was having at work. His boss was always mad at him. Apparently Tom kept saying things to his organization's various customers that got him into trouble. Basically, he would lie. He knew he was a liar. He couldn't help himself. It was not difficult to convince Tom that he was a fake. That was his complaint about himself.

To get his job, Tom lied about his credentials. When his boss inquired about the status of something, Tom would lie if he had to. He told me that he told anywhere from five to thirty little fibs per day. I didn't know if I could believe him. But that was the point.

His explanation for lying was that when he was a kid, his father would frighten him when he did something wrong. It meant that he had to build a defense to avoid his father's wrath. His defense was to lie. Over time, it became very easy to do so. He almost couldn't understand why his boss and peers had a problem with it.

Tom felt conflicted. He was aware that some part of him always wanted to impress people. So he said whatever it took to achieve the mission. The problem, aside from the complaints against him, was that at some level he knew that saying untrue things was not good. He felt shame.

Progress for Tom came as he learned to respect the motivation for lying. He realized that, speaking metaphorically, the little guy in his personality, the subpersonality who told the lies, was just doing what he could in order to be loved. The desire for attention was pure. In its own way, it was sweet. So Tom came to accept this motive and, through increased self-awareness of the conflicted feelings it caused and the consequences of his deceit, to self-censor.

Partial Disclosure

Predictably, when people have a secret—a secret truth or pain or fear—they have to work hard to hide it. And sometimes they feel shame or guilt or just an undercurrent of angst. Believe it or not, sometimes they are not even aware of the feeling they are hiding from. But to survive with this kind of secret, they get into the habit of not saying much. "Partial disclosure" becomes the norm.

There is an insidious aspect to partial disclosure. It can start with one person not being open about their vulnerability. Other people can sense when someone is not being open, and it leads to feelings of mistrust. Then the disease spreads and we have the stuff of office politics: people telling half stories, defending themselves against possible attacks from other partial disclosers. In Chapter 15 we'll look at how a communication style of "full exposure" is the antidote not only to office politics but to fakery as well. We'll see how shining the light on your reality, confident that the truth really will "set you free," relieves you of all the efforts you expend to hide your secret.

Sometimes people don't want to accept their reality because they are afraid that doing so will mean they will stop aspiring to be better. I can think of a man named Sal, who was consistently disappointed that he had never gone far enough in his career. He spent beyond his means, always revealing that he wished he had attained some higher level. I spoke to Sal about just accepting that he had achieved what he had achieved.

His response was clear: "If I accept that, I would lower myself. I would have to admit that I'm in over my head. My world would collapse. I'd become what I am: lazy, greedy, and selfish and, basically, a failure. I would slip into sloth. So, no."

Was Sal right? If we accept that we have failed, does that mean we become a failure? That is the question. And the answer is a clear "no." It is good to accept yourself, all your successes and strengths and your failures and weaknesses. When you do it, you relax. And then, through some eternally ironic quirk of nature, you start to achieve. What seems to happen is that the tension created by the fakery dissipates. You're left with what you really are: somebody with a fear of failure and a hunger to achieve.

Often people tell me they have a particular message they have to give to somebody and they don't know how to say it. They ask for help. And I always say, tell the facts, all the facts.

One client, Eloise, was the leader of a large, award-winning advertising agency. She had a reputation for being creative and bright, but also for being volatile and crabby.

Eloise had a creative team reporting to her that apparently did some work that her company's client strongly disliked. She had to advise the team that their work had to be reconsidered. She was always nervous in cases like this, since creative teams are easily deflated. Unfortunately, Eloise's traditional style in such situations was to sound cold and judgmental. She would tell them outright, "You guys, the client thought your work stunk. I didn't like it either. You've missed the point. It has to be redone."

My advice to Eloise was to disclose fully. That is, don't just tell the client's story, but tell her own, the one behind her crabby remarks, as well. I asked her, "Are you reluctant to tell them you've been nervous?"

"Yes."

"Why?"

"Because they'll get pissed at me for not standing up for them."

"Okay, so why not tell them all that?" I asked. "Why not say, 'I feel awkward telling you this because I'm afraid you will think that I didn't support you. I don't want to deflate your momentum. I also think the client has a point. The demographics don't support the approach you've taken.'"

This was counterintuitive to her. She explained that she didn't like to expose her own vulnerability because it showed signs of weakness.

Ah. That's it for all of us. When we speak to people, we're not inclined to expose ourselves. Instead, we hide our weaknesses in honor of our image. Full exposure means fully including our vulnerabilities in our communication. When there are no secrets, there is nothing to hide.

Owning the Truth

Ultimately, the key to overcoming the feelings that go with being a fake is to "own" the truth that is being hidden. That's not to say it's easy.

First of all, as a coach I have tried to stop using the word *own* in the context of "owning your feelings." Nobody instantly gets the meaning. So, here's a better explanation. When you acknowledge something to yourself, such as that you possess a quality or trait, or you are responsible for some misfortune, you are owning it. Lots of times we become fakes because we are not acknowledging something about ourselves.

The fake, in any of the forms we have talked about, is moving away from or ignoring something that doesn't want to be ignored. The thing being ignored needs to be embraced instead. The crooked stockbrokers were moving away from or ignoring their beliefs about what's fair. The boss who didn't want to confront the consistently tardy employee was ignoring her responsibility to address it. Smokers trying to quit are ignoring their better judgment when they fire up another cigarette. Catherine ignored her fear of being over her head on the job and, as a result, convoluted her communication. Daniel the trainer attempted to ignore his belief that he didn't deserve the applause, and it made him feel conflicted as a result. The list goes on.

Accepting Responsibility and Self-Forgiveness

A client named Marianna had the fake trait. Similar to Catherine and Roxanne, she held onto a deep fear that she wouldn't measure up. In one session, Marianna, who was a very successful salesperson, said that she was very angry that one of her regular customers had decided to go to bid with a large order, rather than just give the order to her. Apparently, the customer just wanted to test the market, to stay in touch with all the supplier possibilities.

I asked Marianna why she was so upset.

"Well," she said, "that bitch was just sending me an underhanded signal that I better not take her business for granted. She knew very well how un-partnership-like it was to do that. I worked like a dog to win her business. And we have taken pretty good care of her. It was a really crabby thing to do. And I'm angry as hell. She had no right—well, she did have the right—but it was totally insensitive to the kind of relationship we've built."

So I reminded her that owning responsibility for misfortune was very important. She got mad at me.

"What in the world do you know about this situation?" she said. "Are you suggesting that I am the cause of this woman's ignorance of professional protocol?"

"Well, let's try something," I said. "You blame her for some aspect of what happens, and then I'll ask you to own the responsibility for it instead. After you 'own' it, you'll be tempted to say, 'Yes, but she should have blah, blah, blah,' but instead I want you to 'own' the fact that she didn't blah, blah, blah, or whatever."

What an interesting interaction! Here's how it went:

MARIANNA: *Well she should have talked to me first!*

ART: *How can you own that she didn't talk to you about it before deciding?*

MARIANNA: *Well, I suppose I haven't really been in touch a lot recently, but that doesn't excuse her from . . .*

ART: *Own it again.*

MARIANNA: *Well, I guess she's bitter because last time we talked, I was a little short with her, but you know, no matter how you cut it, you just don't do that in a partnership.*

ART: *That one, too, Marianna—take responsibility somehow for the fact that she stepped out of the traditional partnership role. How did you deserve it?*

MARIANNA: *Well, I am a little tired of her and I guess it's been showing up lately. And we short shipped the last order, so she's probably disturbed about that, too. Okay, so now I feel terrible.*

At that point, we had made progress. Marianna had moved from anger to a kind of sadness. She was beginning to own something. She was starting to see that she really didn't care about her customer. In fact, Marianna's not caring came before the customer's putting the next piece of business out to bid. Now it was time for her to go all the way.

ART: *Why are you sad?*

MARIANNA: *Because, well, I hate my job. I'm tired of it. And, about that customer, I have been slack lately.*

ART: *Can you forgive yourself for being slack?*

Initially her answer was "no." After all, she had moved from blaming the customer to blaming herself and feeling guilty as a result. Forgiveness is a bigger leap still.

So we pursued why she had apparently been so slack on the job. We uncovered that, deep down, what's really important to Marianna is her son. That's her bigger picture. That's her truth. When she's on the job, she's sort of pretending that she's a dynamo. That was her fakery.

Does this mean she should quit her job? No, it means that by acknowledging to herself that her job indeed comes second to her son, she will put her job into context. She won't have to hide.

This does not mean she will work less hard. It means she won't be conflicted. It doesn't mean she must declare to her boss and the rest of the world that work is really second in her life (that would be professional suicide). It means she does have to declare it to herself.

The Bottom Line

In the end, fakes must come clean, at least with themselves. Everybody referred to in this chapter ultimately got over their angst through some form of self-acceptance. In some cases, it was easy. For example, when the frustrated boss acknowledged that she didn't want to address the late employee because she really didn't want the confrontation, she got some verbal hints for how to disclose fully to the person her concerns and she succeeded in correcting the problem.

The Basic Formula

The basic formula works like this: When there is a split between how you behave and how you think you ought to behave, you feel some kind of angst. One side of the split is usually public and one side is usually private. You may or may not be aware of the private side. The trick is to become aware of the private side and "own" it. Often it is good to own it publicly.

It is no surprise that this split arises in people. I think there is a basic duality that derives from the nature of consciousness. On the one hand, we have the way things are, the "what is," while on the other hand there is the way we want them to be, the "what ought to be." It seems that people go back and forth between operating in these two modes of "is" and "ought."

Businesspeople frequently confuse this distinction. Often in meetings one party will be talking about *what is* the present reality and another will be talking just about *what they want the situation to be*. For example, in my own company we talk about customizing training programs. The marketing leader laments how we just aren't good enough at it yet. An operations person declares he knows how we should do it. The conversation goes around and around until somebody steps in and says: Okay, let's sort out these views in terms of how we are now, how we want to be, and what we have to do to realistically fill the gap.

There are many pairs of words in the English language that reflect these two poles of is and ought. A person can be realistic or optimistic, practical or idealistic, expediency based or principled, descriptive or normative. Indeed, the notion of being a fake itself implies this same tension between what one really is versus what one thinks one ought to be.

Everyone referred to in this chapter wrestled one way or another with the *is–ought* tension. And everyone grew from experiencing what some Buddhists I know would call "holding both." That is, the resolution of our feelings of fakery comes from accepting both "this is my situation" and "I aspire to more." Both are true. This is our humanity.

If You Work with a Fake

Of course, it would be a little presumptuous to go around diagnosing people as "fakes." Indeed, if we are all fakes in some way, then it would be smart to look at ourselves before applying the label to others. Nobody needs to be reminded of their fraudulence. They either want help with it or they don't.

If you work with someone who consciously misleads people, or who exhibits regular bad faith (e.g., doesn't confront when they know they should), or who doesn't feel that the job they have or the work they do or the applause they receive is warranted, or who is not really in touch with their feelings, then:

■ *Be as nonjudgmental as you can be.* That is, don't behave as though their fakery is wrong. It is not up to you to judge them. We all exhibit bad faith or fakery. It's built right into the experience of being awake on the planet. We're talking here about recognizing ourselves, not judging ourselves. When the fakery is on the table, you pretty much have to say, whether to the person or to yourself, "That's okay. Isn't it great to get that out!"

■ *See breaking through fakery as simply making the implicit explicit.* As a matter of definition, people glide over their bad faith without even knowing it. You are merely stopping time, trying to get a person to slow down and become aware of the thoughts between their thoughts.

Shining a light on a certain fakery means to spot inconsistencies in thoughts, statements, values, and behaviors. For example, if someone says Percy is unacceptably late all the time, yet he doesn't talk to Percy about it, you could bring value by asking why. This simple request for clarification points the way. With a certain willingness on the other person's part, you simply have to stay focused on the why until the essential admission of inconsistency pops out.

When people acknowledge an inconsistency and express some discomfort with it, you offer them a gift when you invite them to accept the inconsistency and make commitments around resolving it. In fact, it is good to accept the validity of both perspectives. For example, someone might say, "On the one hand, I have failed at many aspects of my job and so I don't feel I deserve the job, while on the other hand, the people around me treat me like I'm doing a great job—and I feel terrible about the whole mess." That could be your cue to help. In this case you ask what could be done to resolve the inconsistency. The person will find relief from exposing some of her limitations and acknowledging her sincere effort to succeed.

CHAPTER 4

The Attention-Seeker

"See me!"

This is the unspoken plea of attention-seekers. They wave a flag to make sure others stop and notice them. They do not cry out, "Look! Up in the sky!" Nor do they say, "If you happen to look in my direction, I would prefer you to see me in a certain light." No, attention-seekers want a certain judgment from us, and they know how to get it.

Attention-seekers' behavior is linked to whatever they equate with being of value:

- "I did a whole master's thesis on that topic. I'm positive I'm right about this."

- "Well, I used to make several hundred thousand a year, but the economy stopped all that."

- "Look. I've got dozens of places to put my time. Please hurry up with this."

- "I know the CEO. I've had conversations with him. This idea will fly."

In business meetings, they are the ones who always crack jokes or who project an image, as in the examples above, of having academic credibility, financial wherewithal, powerful connections, and so on. They may act as if their minds are on the matter at hand, but what they are really doing is working to draw attention to themselves.

At home, attention-seekers are less covert.

- A husband dances in front of the mirror singing to his wife, "I'm too sexy for my shirt."

- Responding to a playful jab at a dinner gathering, the attention-seeking guest declares, "Aren't I funny? I'm the life of the party!"

- Proud and not afraid to say it, a woman says to her man, "Am I not worthy of respect? Look at all the things I do to help people."

An effort to seek attention does not necessarily indicate attention-seeking behavior. When a woman touches her lover's arm and gently turns his body toward her to say, "I want some attention right now," she is not properly described as an attention-seeker. Nor is a person who raises his voice to be heard in a crowded room. The title of attention-seeker only applies to someone who is doing it most of the time: someone whose overall behavior is best described by their need for validation by others. While their behavior is usually harmless, it can cause problems. For instance, consider the middle manager who takes credit for ideas generated and work done by people under him. How could he possibly ask his workers to take a bow when he has a golden opportunity to take one himself? Or what about the team member who consistently interrupts the flow of dialogue with humor or personal anecdotes? Or the long-winded person who loves to hear himself speak—especially when he has a relatively large audience?

One way or another, attention-seekers get attention, and it's not always without a cost.

Eric sought my help because he knew that underneath his regular attention-seeking efforts, something was amiss. He was a thirty-two-year-old director of consumer marketing in a Fortune 100 company. He was exceptionally bright and very easy to talk to. I was most impressed by his sincerity.

In our sessions together, Eric worked very hard to expose his habit and get to the underlying issue. In one session well into our coaching relationship, he struggled to admit something. He was embarrassed because he was revealing to me the lengths to which he would go to satisfy his need for attention.

He told me that he would occasionally approach shopkeepers and start speaking to them in a foreign language. "Bonjour, pourrais-je avoir . . ." he would say. Then, he would stop himself and say, in English,

"Oh, sorry. Could I have . . ." Eric wanted to jar the salesperson just enough to get her to think, "Wow, this guy must be very smart. He was so lost in thought that he slipped. He realized that he was not speaking my language and he had to adjust. He must be a special fellow."

Eric didn't actually want to buy anything. He would ask for something he knew was not available. He told me he just wanted to be loved.

Perhaps you are thinking Eric must be an extreme example. But I suggest that there is an embarrassing fraudulence behind many attention-seeking efforts. After all, attention-seekers' activities are inherently duplicitous. For instance, while they direct people's attention to something work related, such as the challenges faced in their industry, they are in effect drawing attention to themselves—their department's stellar sales performance in spite of the challenges. Or, outside work, they might discuss the great social needs their favorite charity is meeting, while what they are really pointing out is their own involvement in charitable work. I say the fraudulence is embarrassing because when they stop and admit that something they said was actually intended to draw attention to themselves, they are humbled. They have exposed a raw vulnerability.

Eric's courage to disclose his problem to me was unusual. Attention-seekers usually hide the motives behind their hunger to be seen. Public exposure of the ulterior motive behind attention-seeking would invalidate them. They seek exposure, but not this kind of exposure. They want respect, not shame.

The Behaviors

The motive behind personal flag-waving is pure and innocent. Seeking attention is a positive drive. "It feels good." Attention-seekers, after some dialogue about their behavior, usually get to the core motivation: "I need love." The positive drive is occurring in response to this need.

This drive to get love usually starts in our younger days in a family or school environment, where attention is received only as a reward for performance or appearance. We learn to leverage our strengths. The problem is that we can become dependent on others to supply our self-esteem. Then we become vulnerable when their attention strays. We look for ways in which our strengths can be used to manage that vulnerability. A cat in the jungle, in times of insecurity, responds with her speed, her threatening look, and a terrifying roar. Similarly, a quick-witted fellow in sixth grade may use verbal cleverness to compensate for feelings of rejection.

Some attention-seekers leverage their jobs to satisfy their needs. It's no coincidence that comedians are often attention-seekers. That's why they chose the field. Salespeople may gain personal satisfaction from using their skill of building rapport with customers. Happily, at the same time they are satisfying their employer's needs for sales volume. For many, attention-seeking is their primary means of self-expression. Some people are very successful as a result of gaining the notice of others. Compare an executive with less skill but loads of attention-seeking charm with an executive with more skill but a self-effacing manner. Which one is likely to be promoted?

Consider the diversity of attention-seeking behavior by looking at these real-life examples:

- Kim is an attention-seeker who "acts out" in her department at a communications company when she feels disconnected from her boss. She gets political with her colleagues by uncovering people's secrets and then, to stir things up, telling them to others. Ultimately the boss has to step in. Kim has achieved her goal. Like a child in kindergarten, she has caught the teacher's eye. She is not conscious of the purpose of her efforts.

- Anytime he has been romantically rejected, Robert, a creative copywriter, tells his colleagues little fibs that demonstrate his prowess with women. This behavior compensates for the insecurity and pain of rejection.

- Gary, a lead salesman in a plastics company, gets more playful at meetings in direct proportion to his sales volume. When sales are high, the jokes fly. He is saying, "Look at me. Look at how well I'm doing." When sales are low, the jokes are grounded. The playful pattern is broken by the fear of rejection.

- Mike, the president of a high-tech company, projects an image of enhanced spirituality. Ostensibly, he is devout and even self-effacing. In fact, he is looking for the payback of being considered wise. This validates him.

■ Karen, vice president of a property development company, talks a lot. She is very articulate. But people think she hogs the floor. She admits she likes people to hear her intelligent comments. It makes her feel respected.

■ Mark, a senior vice president of a telecommunications company, gets a thrill from attending the meetings of his various junior vice presidents' salespeople. He likes to shake people up. He is loud and hypercritical. People think he is insensitive and arrogant. He is willing to risk such a judgment in order to project an image of being powerful, strategic, and effective.

■ Deborah gets attention by asking her peers for their insights into her problems. Before a meeting starts, she presents a challenge—a business or personal problem—to attendees who arrive early, and sits back while they contribute their ideas. She absorbs all the attention, but rarely implements what she hears—saved by the start of the meeting, don't you know?

Not only does the behavior vary from person to person but there are also variations within the behavior of a single attention-seeker, based on such factors as stress level, mood, level of insecurity, and the audience. A kind of supply-and-demand dynamic also comes to life: When the supply of attention goes down, demand for attention goes up a corresponding amount.

The Problem

If people have labeled you an attention-seeker, you may feel they are being unfair. After all, how can they be sure that your motive isn't to draw attention to yourself but simply to the thing you are talking about? Only you can know your motives. But if their claim makes you curious, or perhaps defensive, you can explore the motives behind your alleged attention-seeking behavior by exploring your emotions.

Attention-seekers usually feel rejection keenly and are affected by it more than the average bear. That's why they work so hard to seek our notice. When the support is not there, they hurt. This is one of the reasons you might want to work on the matter. I've never had someone call me to say, "I am an attention-seeker and, darn it, I want to stop." Instead, people look for help concerning their mild pangs of anxiety. Only after we get acquainted in our coaching sessions does the topic of attention-seeking arise.

Some clients admit that being busy waving their flag makes them less effective on the job. That makes sense. In any kind of business, people are attempting to reach goals efficiently. Attention-seekers, diverters of attention by definition, ever so briefly run counter to this core business activity. Not surprisingly, when attention-seekers look back after their habit fades, they often remark on how much their personal productivity has improved.

Except for the most committed hermit, people have to, and want to, interact with others. Otherwise, life could be pretty lonely. Relating to people is most convivial when the relating goes both ways. You are involved with me, and I with you. We give of ourselves in some way when we engage with others and they give in return. But when attention-seekers are doing their thing, they are not really playing by these rules. Theirs is a one-sided game. The dynamic is inequitable. They rarely validate the other party as much as they solicit validation. As a family doctor friend of mine put it, "Show-offs are generally resented, even when they are good performers, because they do not allow others an opportunity to exhibit."

As I'm sure is also true of many of you, I regularly interact with service providers, privately and in business. I meet lots of strangers: hotel workers, tradespeople, waitstaff, cab drivers, nurses, retail store employees. Some of these people are obviously eager to talk about themselves. Ask a simple question, and out pours an overview of their present life circumstances and plans for the future. In these situations I find myself wondering whether their behavior is a sign of high self-esteem or of a narcissism that's getting out of hand.

I am slowly learning to assess whether someone—a person in my day-to-day life, outside of coaching relationships—is an attention-seeker by using the equal-time technique. I ask myself whether this person dedicates as much time to me as they expect me to dedicate to them. Is there a two-way dynamic here? Or is it really just about the other person? Do I sense authenticity, such that the person seems to care about me? Many attention-seekers often don't give equal time. They are more focused on themselves.

The Fix

In most cases, solving problems related to attention-seeking does not mean curtailing the attention-seeking behavior itself. As mentioned above, some people find great success and bring great value to the world through their strengths—and those strengths happen to serve a dual purpose: validation for themselves and productivity for their organization. Millions of attention-seekers fully accept themselves as that type of person, as they should.

But sometimes attention-seekers want to tackle various aspects of the pattern. A colleague of mine, who was working on his own attention-seeking tendencies, wanted to change his behavior so that he could address his need for attention in a more honest way. His traditional approach to gaining attention was to think of a topic he could use to justify sitting down with me in the office for a few minutes. It would be any topic that fit under the heading of our mutual professional concerns. What he really wanted, though, was just to affiliate. Ultimately he concluded that coming up with a topic for the sake of affiliating was dishonest.

At his suggestion, we agreed that he would simply announce a craving to affiliate. Now he comes to me and says, "Got a minute? I need some affiliation." We smile at the shared understanding and spend a few minutes together. Starting a dialogue this way may seem inelegant, but it is honest.

A client named Jean asked her teammates to support her in a special way when she was feeling needy. Her traditional response to insecurity was to start to whine. She hated this tendency in herself. People teased her for it. It worked for her at one level, but she just didn't like what it said about her. She asked her colleagues, when they noticed she was "acting out," to assume that she was feeling insecure. Their commitment was to point out her behavior and as nonjudgmentally as possible talk through what was making her insecure. She told me this kept her honest. And it seemed to work. She had very supportive coworkers.

Both of these people had a fairly healthy or mature outlook concerning their attention-seeking. I believe people do become less needy of external attention as they mature emotionally. Sometimes, however, the coaching relationships need to drill down a little deeper. When people approach me as a coach regarding their insecurity, my mission is to help them put a face on the pain.

John, an extraordinarily successful real estate agent in Manhattan, was very curious about what that face might be in his case. His challenge was that whenever he lost a sale he felt completely deflated. He said it had been getting worse as the years went by.

John and I worked together for eight sessions. He was a very hard worker. It seemed that whatever task he undertook, including addressing the insecurity that drove him, he did it marvelously. But he had such pain! Over time we built a list of key moments in his life.

Picture two young parents having their first child. The child was John. The parents were totally inexperienced with nurturing babies and raising kids. At the time of his birth the mother was an unemployed waitress and the father an apprentice electrician. When they got home from the hospital with baby Johnny, a whole new stress was introduced into their lives. They were simply unprepared to be good parents.

Baby Johnny's crying was the father's biggest frustration. He couldn't deal with it. The sleepless nights seemed to be going on for months on end. The mother was experiencing postpartum depression and her incessantly irritable husband was thin support. For the first few years of his life, Johnny lived in a very tense household.

At night, after putting Johnny to bed, the mother would turn out the light and go watch television. Johnny would start to cry shortly thereafter. She would go into his room, pick him up, and the crying would stop. After a few months of this routine went by, the father had what he thought was a good idea. "You run to him so soon!" he said. "He's got you conditioned. Let him cry a little. You'll see; he'll go to sleep." So they tried the experiment.

Johnny cried for several minutes but eventually went to sleep. The father said, "See? It worked." Although she hated the crying noise, the mother learned to accept that he would usually cry through it.

As for Johnny, he had an instinctive craving and the craving was not satisfied. These very early years became a metaphor for his home life. Unmet cravings were the name of the game.

Cut to kindergarten. When Johnny's mother went to see the teacher, she was told that Johnny seemed smart, but he was very rough with the other children. He also never settled down at nap time and at story time he was a little disruptive. "He's very busy looking for attention," the teacher said. Johnny's mother said, "That's our Johnny."

Now cut to the parent-teacher interview in sixth grade. By this point, Johnny was the class clown. In this case, the teacher didn't really have a problem with Johnny's behavior. Sure, he was disruptive, but he was also a delightful boy. "He volunteers to sharpen pencils at recess," she said, expressing the pleasure she took from having Johnny in her class.

Johnny was growing up to be quite a nice person. He seemed affable. He was outgoing and playful. He knew just how to make his friends laugh, and he did it all the time. He was not particularly happy at home, however. He craved more time from his father. But Daddy was always out, going to people's homes to fix their wires. And when he came home, he was tired. Johnny would watch his father watch television. He would see his father laugh at the funny shows. He would hear his parents argue. He would watch his mother running around the house dealing with his sister and brother.

Jumping way ahead now to early in John's career, it was clear to those around him that John would be a superstar salesman. He had a unique ability to sense when customers liked him and when they didn't. When he got the feeling that he was disliked, or that the customer didn't like what he was recommending, John was able to respond quickly— sometimes, it seemed, even before the customer was aware of her own opinion.

As one successful year followed another, John had lots of opportunities to explain his success and try to teach it to other people. It was subtle, but here's what he was sure of. "You have to watch people's faces and body movements to know what they are thinking," he would say. "Whatever is on their minds is revealed in their body language. And when they don't feel good, you've got to make them feel good. The trick to that is to give them what they want. If they like their idea better, you must go with their idea. If they are bored, you must not drag them through all the details. Go where the customer is! Be the customer!"

In more reflective times, John knew what explained his success. He told me early in our relationship, "You know, I never ever got the attention that I wanted when I was a kid—from either of my parents. My father was always out, or at home watching TV and drinking beer, and my mother was always taking care of my brother and sister. My sister is mentally handicapped, by the way, so she needed a lot of attention. Anyway, I did get pretty skilled at reading people. I guess it was because I was so hungry for the least glimmer of connection—anything would do. A smile, for example—I remember just wanting a smile."

His problem, he said, was that in spite of all the interpersonal skills he had developed naturally, he could still feel the need to please. And he didn't like it. There was something bugging him underneath it all. Whenever he lost a sale, the thing that was bothering him became more intense.

Our work together was to find out what was on his mind.

"What do you think it is?" I asked.

"Well, I know it's all related. My skills come from my need to please. When I do not please someone, it hurts. I guess I fear that hurt. I guess I still hurt. But that doesn't make it go away."

Indeed. An intellectual understanding of all the links does not remove the emotional anguish. Somehow, one must deal with things from within the emotions, not from outside. So that's what we did.

"John, let's look at the rejection you feel when you lose a sale. Tell me about that."

"Well, it just happened recently. It's still fresh on my mind. The customer chose a facility being sold by my biggest competitor. I blew it."

"How does that make you feel?"

"Lousy. It's like, for some reason, they didn't like me. It hurts."

I asked him to close his eyes. I walked him through my preferred exercise for getting people who stay at an intellectual level to connect with their feelings. "Where in your body do you feel the hurt?" I asked him.

John pointed to his chest.

"What does it feel like?"

"It feels tight."

Tightness in the chest is where a lot of people feel their rejection. "Feel it there for a short while, John. Let's go with it." I noticed that John was holding his breath, letting it go, and then holding it again. That's what people do. They brace themselves tightly in order to keep the hurt in. "Breathe, John. It's okay. What are you feeling?"

John winced. "I feel sad. Very sad. They didn't love me. I wanted that business so badly. I tried everything I knew. And I was sure they liked me. And then they said no!"

John was connecting the business matter with his need to be liked or loved. For him, what he did every day was about being loved. When he sold real estate, he was selling himself.

That's one problem faced by attention-seekers. By making their self-esteem dependent on the love of others, they set themselves up for huge pain when they don't get it. Most attention-seekers who get help ultimately learn to derive their esteem needs more from themselves. That's where John and I were heading in this dialogue.

"Breathe, John."

His exhalation opened him up. Out came sobbing cries. John had been holding in pain for an awfully long time. But he only cried for ten minutes, busily managing the tissues required to protect him from being totally embarrassed. But that's okay; the process of facing one's pain is gradual. After such a cry, defenses are down, and feelings, partially spent, are exposed and accessible. It was a good moment for John to make connections between behavior and feelings. John had the opportunity to integrate his emotions into his self-understanding.

"John, what does it feel like when you let it out like that?"

He got out a four-word answer before bursting back into tears. "I feel so small!"

Another couple of minutes passed. "Tell me more."

"It's like I'm alone. It's an emptiness."

"Can you feel that emptiness now?"

"Yes, it's as clear as day."

"Good, John. Let's rest in that emptiness for a while. In this room. Right now. Feel it. Close your eyes for me, and feel it."

He complied.

"Assume that this emptiness, John, is part of you. Observe it as part of you. It is not who you are, but it is a part of you. It may be your motivation on the job. It has been with you all your life."

John sat there, slouched in his chair, quiet for several minutes. Periodically, he would wince and look as if he was about to cry. Then the wave would pass and he would be thoughtful again.

He looked at me with a resigned expression. He shook his head and said, "It's amazing. It feels like all my life I have been followed by this shadow of pain. It explains so much! Everything I have done comes from this pain. My successes were caused by it. My failures reminded me of it. I feel like I'm just so simple. It's sad. It's so simple."

After a slight pause, he curled his lip, about to be playfully sarcastic. "I'm just an asshole. A programmed machine. Everything looked so complicated but it's all very simple. We're like cattle grazing the planet. Not much more."

John's insights aside, he was integrating his feelings into his worldview. This was progress. He was learning to accept himself for what he was. Over time, and several more conversations, that self-acceptance made him much less vulnerable to the ups and downs of his sales career.

At one session, John wondered whether getting in touch with his emotions would cause him to lose his skills and motivation for selling. I said I couldn't be sure about the motivation, but I was positive that his skills would not diminish. His acute awareness of others' thoughts and feelings was his. It may have evolved from a need for love that was never fulfilled. But it was a gift. John even volunteered, "There are two sides to every coin; my parents may have starved me, but look at where I am now."

It has been four years since John and I completed our sessions. But we still exchange e-mails. He is now the CEO of a different real estate company. He only gets involved in the "monster deals" but he still gets to use his people skills as a leader. He does not consider himself an attention-seeker any more. He knows that the programming is in there, and the finely tuned acumen is always at his disposal; even the feeling of emptiness is accessible to him. But, as he puts it, "I'm not so raw."

If You Work with Attention-Seekers

Your goal is probably to keep them motivated but to "turn them down" a bit.

Very few attention-seekers are prepared to admit what's going on. Remember that you can't just tell someone they are an attention-seeker. After all, you don't have access to their private motivations. Nobody likes to be labeled. You can never win the argument. Don't be hurtful by labeling.

If somebody does admit that he is frequently busy seeking attention, you can validate the motivation. There is nothing inherently wrong with the desire to be seen. In fact, it could be argued that attention-seeking is a very healthy response to the world. The only problem—and he will probably be prepared to admit to it—is that sometimes he goes too far (consuming valuable time, taking risks with their team's image, being hurtful to others through humor). So with the admission comes the opportunity to negotiate. And with increased awareness through ongoing dialogue comes an improved ability to control impulses.

If someone does not readily admit to the negative effects of their behavior, and you need the behavior to change, then don't go to the topic of motive. Stay on the topic of behavior: "When you do that," you can tell her, "it has this effect. Please try not to do that, so that we can avoid the effect." Consider the possibility that if attention-seekers really "push your buttons," it may be because in some way you see yourself in their behavior. And you may not like your own attention-seeking impulses. Take a look in the mirror; insecurity drives us all.

CHAPTER 5

The Victim

My wife, Joan, just came in from picking up her car at the dealership where she had taken it for repairs. She was angry. "They were pathetically late again," she told me. Joan always gets frustrated when she has repairs performed there because the car is never ready at the time promised. This was a busy time for her and somebody else's tardiness had thrown a wrench into her day.

They had promised her she could pick up the car at noon. Having been burned before, she waited until 12:20 P.M. and then phoned to check in. The service adviser said, "Sure. They're just finishing up. Come right in."

When she arrived at 12:30, the service adviser again said, "They're just finishing up. Please take a seat in the waiting room."

Every ten minutes or so she peeked at the service bay to see if the car was still there. At 1:00 she saw the car drive out of the lot. She went to the service adviser, who told her, "Yup, all done; looks like he's just taking it out for a test drive." When Joan expressed some frustration, the adviser said, "Sorry about the wait, ma'am, but we like to test drive the cars to make sure everything is running properly." So she went back to the waiting room.

Now, here's the kicker. She hadn't noticed the car return, and it was now 1:30. She went back to the service reception area and was surprised to see that the car was being washed. "I want my car!" she said to the man. "You told me yourself it would be ready by noon and now it's 1:30. I've been waiting here an hour!"

"We wash the cars when we're done with them, ma'am. It's a regular service."

"That's nice, but it's late," she said. "I really don't have time for a car wash. I have to go. And I resent your not getting me out of here faster."

"I've been one mechanic short all morning, ma'am," the service adviser said, getting a little defensive. "And people without appointments showed up and . . ."

Joan must have looked at him as though he were crazy. He obviously saw in her expression that it would not be smart to continue. He put his hands up to show he understood and said, "I know, I know, you don't want to hear it."

Who Is the Victim?

My wife was definitely a victim in this piece, but not the kind of victim we want to talk about in this chapter. We're more interested in victims like the service adviser. His job was, among other things, to please the customer. He did not. Rather than acknowledge his failure, he avoided the blame. "It's not my fault," he might as well have said. "How did I know I'd be one mechanic short? What can I do—drag him out of his bed and make him work? How am I supposed to control the schedule when the unexpected happens? I'm the victim here. I'm not God, you know. I can't control what I can't control."

When we say someone is a victim, in the psychological sense, we are referring to that person's marked tendency to attribute problems externally. Rather than saying, "I failed to avoid this mess," victims say, "Responsibility for this mess cannot be attributed to me." Victims are adept at letting themselves off the proverbial hook. It doesn't help in business, where we are always stretching ourselves to achieve more and more, when a member of a team regularly lets himself off the hook for not coming through. Same thing at home.

The service adviser did indeed draw attention to how he was not to blame for the problem. He was using the busyness of his day to explain why he was not able to satisfy the customer's desire to get her car back on time. He attributed the problem not to himself but to factors external to him. He felt he was being attacked and attempted to defend himself. His job was, among other things, to please the customer. He did not. Rather than acknowledging this, he avoided the blame.

Of course, we can't know what was going on in his head at the time. But let's speculate. He told my wife a time and the time elapsed. He didn't come through on his word. He knew that she was frustrated, and he knew he could have done something to speed things up for her, such as asking her if bypassing the road test or canceling the wash would be okay, but he didn't.

Lies We Tell Ourselves

The blunt truth is too painful for victims, so they shift the blame away from where they suspect it belongs. The thing being hidden—even vaguely from themselves—is the belief that the blame rests at least partly on their shoulders. The service adviser probably knew he could have avoided my wife's frustrations. Perhaps out of a misguided desire to please, he didn't expose this knowledge.

People normalize victim behavior so the lies become easy to tell. They become accustomed to telling them. Employees in some industries are put in situations where they have to adopt a victim stance. For example, the high-tech industry sells leading-edge products and services that, by their very nature, have not yet been perfected. Customer-contact people in this community often really are between a rock and a hard place.

Speaking realistically, service advisers at car dealerships do have a very tough job. Sometimes they can keep their promises, and sometimes they just can't. Management pressures them into making promises for any one of many reasons—mostly pertaining to competitive survival. So they promise things will be done by a certain time. But Murphy's Law comes into effect, and things go awry. They could spend half their days owning blame for things simply because their job forces them to give their word when their word can't be consistently fulfilled. They avoid the angst by deflecting the blame. The same is true of many work situations today, where employees are often asked to juggle a ridiculous amount of work. It is so tempting to blame reality in such situations.

But people normalize victim behavior when it isn't mandated, too. They find themselves sliding down a slippery slope of deflecting blame. Once they get away with doing this a few times, they learn it works, and then it becomes a habit. Some tradespeople have reputations of simply never being on time. I once saw a handyman's truck that proclaimed in big letters a list of what made him special. "I always arrive at the promised time!" the top bullet said. The next one said, "When late, I always call."

Owning Blame

The tendency to avoid blame is pretty strong in most of us. After all, we are on pretty shaky ground. Our lives are full of stress, we are constantly asked to change, we are being judged by others incessantly, we have insecurities we've been wrestling with since childhood, it's very hard to make a living in the modern economy—why would we ever want to stop what we're doing and say, "Go ahead, make it worse"? Victim thinking is very tempting. Resisting the temptation takes courage.

Most arguments are struggles for responsibility. When you fight with colleagues, you are probably trying to get them to take responsibility. They, on the other hand, want you to take responsibility. If the argument is something that has yet to happen, it is about assuming accountability for a task. If it is about something that has already happened, it is about finding someone to blame.

The way out of this vicious circle is to learn to own blame. What does it mean to own blame?

I think of playing army when I was a kid. If somebody shot me, he would yell, "I got you—you're dead." If I accepted his claim, I had to make a dramatic fall and then was out of the game for a while. It was an undesirable outcome (unless I wanted to go home anyway). But it was not necessary to accept the claim. An option was to argue, "No way! You couldn't have got me. I was still behind the tree!" If you said it at the right volume and with enough certainty, the bullet might be dodged.

Owning blame means taking the bullet. Why don't people take bullets? Well, obviously, bullets hurt. Also, when people work in an environment where no one takes the blame, why be the only one who does?

Once again we go back to childhood. When we are feeling insecure as kids and somebody says we are flawed, we feel even more insecure. Criticism and blame remind us of feeling small. They invalidate us. Rather than strengthening us, they tend to move us closer to what we fear: total insecurity. On the other hand, if we have lots of security, if we trust that we are loved by someone unconditionally, if our self-esteem is high and we have the beliefs that we are able and worthy, then criticism is less penetrating. We're less likely to take the victim route.

Victims do tend to have lower self-esteem. With low self-esteem comes the sometimes hidden belief "I am not okay." When the question of blame arises, there is an instantaneous, habituated response: "I mustn't let that in—it will make me even less okay."

The Victim Response

The act of deflecting responsibility can be one of quiet desperation. Often a victim will move from simple facts to generalizations, bad feelings, and blame for the feelings. Let's say Bill, a colleague of mine, doesn't get a report to me on time. For Bill this can become a study in who held him up, how they tend to always hold things up, how they hold everything up, and how upsetting it is that they always hold everything up. It's just not fair, darn it.

People do tend to generalize when they feel insecure. And since insecurity is at the heart of victim behavior, generalization is common among victims. Let's look at a scenario involving a victim and his boss.

Jamie works as a speechwriter for Victoria, the CEO of a large financial services organization. Jamie has been in this role for six months. He is a good writer with excellent credentials. He is also a little insecure in his job. Getting it was a big step in his career and he doesn't want to blow it.

Jamie still has not quite absorbed Victoria's style, so things are not as smooth between them as he would like. When it's time to write a speech, Victoria assigns a topic and gives Jamie some insight into her position. But he doesn't quite get all the nuances. Jamie comes to Victoria with his first draft of a speech she is to deliver at a dinner the next night to a group of key executives from client organizations.

"Victoria, here is a draft of the capitalization speech," Jamie says. "I was hoping you would give it a look before I start polishing." He hands her the hard copy.

Scanning the first paragraph, Victoria says, "No. This opening won't do. I told you that we have to start on a light note. This sounds too negative."

"But I spoke with Robert about the mood of the group and got the feeling that a lot of people are frustrated about the market and how the company is doing, so I didn't want to go too light, if you know what I mean."

"Sure, but you've overcompensated."

"Okay, I'll change it."

After they have discussed the rest of the draft, Jamie leaves Victoria's office. At lunchtime, when he runs into Victoria's assistant, with whom he has become friendly, he says, "I could kill Robert. He specifically said that the audience for tomorrow's speech wanted to hear nothing but the facts. He said they blame Victoria for the mess and anything that sounded defensive would only further anger them. I hate receiving mixed instructions. This happens a lot around here. We should have a system where Victoria and Robert get their strategies straight before assigning me speeches."

From Jamie's view, the heaviness at the start of the speech was not his fault. It was Robert's fault. Jamie is frustrated. He wants to change the system so this doesn't happen again.

From Victoria's point of view, the start of the speech is obviously too heavy. She doesn't care about the cause. She thinks Jamie sounded like a victim as soon as he said he was following Robert's input. But she acknowledges that he did change his tune quickly when he said he would change the speech.

The assistant tells one of her colleagues later, "Victoria is going to eat him alive. I can tell. He comes up with all these explanations for why things go off the rails. Then he starts complaining. He doesn't do it in front of her much, but she'll figure it out. When she does, she'll move him out. He'll never know why."

The assistant was onto something. People don't like victims. They can smell victim behavior and it turns them off. In service roles, victims are poison. Customers crave the feeling that somebody is on the case. They are repulsed by people who are supposed to be on the case but let themselves off the hook.

Victims Generalize

The tendency of victims to move from facts to generalizations is often part of the blame-deflection process. In these cases a fact that appears to insinuate them gets attributed to some other person or group of people who, the victim is eager to point out, is "always" at fault. Then the victim refers to that recurring fault as frustrating.

There are two types of victim behavior, both of which usually employ generalizations. In one type of victim behavior, people say the equivalent of "it's not my fault." In this case, as in the previous example, responsibility for misfortune is deflected to someone else. Generalizations are sometimes added, in some cases to support the defense, as in "we always do it that way," and in others to explain the frustration that is felt, as in "you always do that." Probably half of all victim responses are of the "it's not my fault" type.

In the other type of victim behavior, the "woe is me" response is used, in an effort to communicate that specific bad things have seemingly conspired to make a situation very difficult. "So no wonder this has happened." This response allows a little blame in but manages to keep most of it out by soliciting the compassion of the other party. For example, when the service adviser who dealt with my wife began to say that he was short one mechanic all morning, he was saying, "You can't really blame me, ma'am. A generalized view of the morning will show you that I am free of blame."

"But It's True!"

You might be thinking, "Hold on here. Aren't there legitimate reasons for why these unfortunate things occur? Can't a person explain what went wrong without being labeled a victim?" My response is that we are not talking about the truth of the victim's claims. We are talking about whether people hold themselves accountable for success. When people allow themselves to attribute blame away from themselves, they are less productive. By letting themselves off the hook, they justify not tackling problems that arise.

When a victim attempts something and runs into a problem—a trigger problem idiosyncratic to that victim—she will likely let herself off the hook with a "woe is me" or "it's not my fault." In this sense, truth gets in the way. It presents the reason for failure before failure occurs. With predicted failure comes a cloud of helplessness and resignation. But on the more hopeful side, with ownership of the mission come refreshed attempts to achieve.

I once did an adventure exercise in which I had to climb more than twenty feet up a pole to get to a platform. I made the first fifteen feet but then found myself quite frightened. The last five feet seemed incredibly treacherous. Complete resignation was the only thing on my mind. I was visualizing how I would explain my early failure in the program. It was clear in my mind how absolutely stupid it was to climb a pole to a platform. "What is this going to prove anyway!" I was, as far as I was concerned, done. I could have just let go of the pole, relying on the safety harness to get me out of the mess I was in. After all, I thought, "This is stupid. I am not interested in this. This is just some jock's game for other jocks."

I was a victim. By organizing my thoughts for why I could not achieve the goal, I was giving in to them. However, the voices at the bottom of the pole were louder than the ones in my head. I made it over the top.

I have always been intrigued by the polarity of "no excuses allowed" versus "be realistic." Victims, except perhaps when they overgeneralize, can be very realistic. It is one advantage they have. Realistically, the service adviser taking care of my wife did have a problem that day. Jamie, the speechwriter, may have been appropriately influenced by Robert. I, not being an athletic kind of guy, may in fact have been sorely underprepared for the pole-climbing exercise. Shouldn't there be a role for realism? Am I a victim for stating the facts?

The distinction is that victim thinking occurs when the difficulty or unfairness of reality is used as an escape clause. As a manager, I can handle people explaining what went wrong, particularly when they appear to sincerely regret the failure. And if they played a role in the failure itself, if they actually made a mistake, I like to hear them own it. What bothers me, and others, about victims is that they use their explanation of what went wrong to let themselves off the hook. What infuriates people about victims is the denial of culpability.

One problem victims face is that over time in a single environment their complaints become consistent. This confines them to unhappiness. Then not only do they incur the dislike of those around them but they also find themselves in a rut. They don't do anything about the problem because, of course, it's not their fault. It is real, but it is not their problem. It is the fault of things like the organization, management, the lack of team spirit, inadequate systems, constant change, flawed products and services—anything. Again, the tendency to attribute the blame frees them of responsibility and the inclination to keep trying.

Victim Thinking

Consistent and persistent complaints lead to the victim label. And real problems lead to the complaints. But why is one person likely to respond as a victim to real problems while another is not?

Role models have an impact. Victim thinking can be contagious. When people join a new corporate culture, they often adopt the majority's response to responsibility. In organizations that can be said to have a blame culture, new people pick up the disease.

Victim orientation can also come from personal insecurity. Life experiences can leave a person feeling fundamentally insecure. For example, if parents don't create a feeling in a child of trust, the child may grow up feeling vulnerable. Indeed, children need to know that Mommy or Daddy or Caregiver is totally reliable. That trust creates a foundation for healthy self-esteem. Imagine being a child of unreliable parents! Unfortunately, most kids—maybe all kids—feel some degree of insecurity. Perhaps it is just part of our humanity. We can't always get what we want. The feeling of insecurity, though it comes in degrees, is universal. As I said, we can all fall into victim mode.

Insecurity can also come from external sources such as the work environment. For example, people who work in organizations that have had to lay people off or are quick to dismiss people are a little paranoid about the reactions they may run into. Also, working for a boss who tends to invalidate his employees can create feelings of insecurity. It's ironic that some bosses bemoan the presence of victims on their team so loudly and regularly that they create a perfect environment for victim thinking to get out of hand. They blame; they generalize; they judge.

Agency

Addressing victim thinking can be done organizationally and, of course, at the individual level. Both challenges must start with education. Discussing topics such as what victim thinking looks like and where it comes from is critical. The goal is to get victims to be more like agents.

Agency is the opposite of victim thinking. The word pertains to being an "agent of change" or a cause agent. When a chemical agent is added to a substance, it causes change. Whether at work or at home, when agency is added to a problem, people move.

In addition to education, organizations need three ingredients for improving their sense of agency:

1. They need role models, preferably among their leaders, who demonstrate the desired style of thinking and behavior.
2. They need to elevate the self-esteem of employees, so there is less insecurity in the organization.
3. They need to "talk it up," so that people make both playful and supportively critical references to victim thinking.

Elevating the self-esteem of employees is obviously a difficult mission. Many managers are a long way from understanding how badly they deflate their employees. Effectively supporting their people calls for an infusion of compassion and patience into their day-to-day style. One key is to stay focused on facts rather than being judgmental. When failure occurs, and there is an honest agent-like attitude toward it, leaders need to applaud effort rather than find blame. Leaders need their people to feel that half the job is having the right attitude.

Leaders must be careful not to say, "We have a culture of victim thinking because we have a bunch of victims on staff." Instead, they must say and own that they have failed to create the desired nonvictim culture. Then they must be agents and do what it takes to make the correction. Leaders are just as responsible for the victim-like behavior of their people as are the victims themselves. Both parties must attack the problem.

Becoming More Agent-Like

Let's assume that you have seen yourself in this chapter. For you to become more agent-like, there are three things you can do.

First, while in the middle of a challenging task, manage your personal mental chatter. When going into a victim mode, listen to what is running through your head. Catch yourself uttering the equivalent of "poor me" or "it's not my fault." Replace that chatter with "I can do this." Resist the temptation to form conclusions about your ability to achieve a goal and instead stay focused on what can still be done.

Looking back on a failed task or problem situation, be sure to include yourself in the description of what went wrong. By definition, you were involved and the problem occurred. Don't pretend otherwise. See blame as a problem of communication with others and within yourself. You may have failed to get someone to think or act differently or you may not have anticipated problems that could have been predicted.

Second, explore the possibility that there is little to gain from blaming. Blaming feels like a useful endeavor since, after all, finding the source of a problem usually means that a solution is at hand. But pointing to what went wrong is often nothing but a distraction from admitting culpability and finding a solution.

If you have a problem, or are frustrated by a matter, you have apparently not fixed it. You may wish to describe who is "doing you wrong," but the real point is that you have not communicated with somebody such that they help you make things work. If you stop to point a finger, you have done just that: stopped. Instead, observe the facts, compare where you are with where you want to be, make a plan to close the gap, and act.

When you stop taking the time to assign blame, you take on a lot of responsibility. That responsibility is what you fear. You have the illusion that taking responsibility opens the door to personal failure. In fact, it is the taking of responsibility that is important, perhaps more so than achieving the goal itself.

A client once told me, "I am insecure because my mother did not attend to my needs. I have spent many years feeling anger and have never been able to kick it." It took some time for us to establish that while his mother may indeed have not attended to his needs and could be blamed for his insecurity, in the present he was responsible for his feelings. He had to get his head around the idea that he was stuck in the blame. He had to move into the possibility that "I am now responsible for what I do with my life."

For a certain number of people who wrestle with a victim-thinking habit, admitting personal responsibility for misfortune leads to taking failure personally. Unfortunately, once the thing they avoided through blame is actually admitted, whoever helped them reach that insight suddenly receives a sarcastic "Thanks a lot! Now I feel terrible with each of my failures."

Third, forgive yourself. As I said earlier, low self-esteem can lead you to own personal blame and consequently feel bad about yourself. Such a feeling stems from a value judgment you make. Rather than attending to the facts, you are saying what the facts mean. And when you extend a short series of facts into a generalized pattern, and then make a judgment about yourself, problems set in. Just as leaders need to resist the temptation to make value judgments, you need to avoid judging yourself.

Let's look more closely at this phenomenon.

Personalization and Self-Forgiveness

Gloria was a victim who worked toward agency. Along the way she fell into personalization. Once she learned to accept that she was accountable, she began to experience what she was initially afraid of: remorse over her failures. The key was for her to own the accountability and then to resist the temptation to judge herself for failing to achieve the impossible. Instead of giving in to judgment, she had to just keep moving toward her goals.

Gloria worked for me. She was a close personal friend. She had previously worked in a government organization, and I knew that bringing her on board was a risk. She would be moving from a relatively bureaucratic enterprise to an entrepreneurial one, and I wasn't sure the switch would go smoothly. Philosophically, the value systems were different. Whereas my entrepreneurial organization was interested in the three goals of optimal efficiency, optimal customer satisfaction, and optimal sales, her previous government job was focused on—well, different things. But Gloria was my friend and she was exceptionally bright. I knew she could learn.

In those days of my career, I was delivering small-group training sessions four out of five days, most weeks of the year. As a matter of fact, I was the small organization's product. Almost every day of the year, assuming I was working locally as opposed to out of town, I would wake up in the morning, take a shower, dress, then go downstairs to my mailbox and remove the training manuals for that day's session, which had been put there for me overnight. This was the most efficient way to do business. On Tuesday, I would be with one company and on Wednesday, I would be with another. On Tuesday, my little team would be finalizing and printing the manuals for the Wednesday session. At the end of Tuesday they would deliver the manuals for Wednesday to my mailbox. This routine worked well for the team.

I brought Gloria on board to lead the team. After all, I was not able to work on the company's evolution because I was busy working for clients. It is a common problem in small training and consulting organizations. I needed someone I could trust to run the company while I was out serving clients.

One morning about a week into Gloria's arrival, I went to the mailbox to grab the package of training manuals for that day's session. There was nothing there—no manuals. This was a big problem for me. Without a set of handouts for that day's session, I would be naked. Not only would I not have a document to guide me through the session, but the participants would not have a permanent learning tool into which they could record what was relevant to them.

I stood at my front door feeling concerned and curious. Gloria was new in the job. Could there have been some minor miscommunication? Maybe she had the handouts in her car or something.

I called her. She was in her car on her way to work. "Gloria, I'm going to XYZ client today for the session on management coaching, but there are no manuals in my mailbox," I said.

"I know," she replied. "Yesterday was extraordinarily busy. It was amazing."

I paused, thinking she would then explain the backup plan or the whereabouts of the day's training manuals. After a few seconds, I said, "Okay. But the manuals for today—where are they?"

"That's what I mean," she said. "We were busy yesterday; we couldn't do them."

"Why didn't you tell me?"

"I assumed Linda told you. She said she would be talking to you, and I trusted her to do it. Didn't she tell you?"

"No," I said.

I had to laugh to myself. My company helped groups of people learn about things like taking accountability, and I had hired a victim to run it. Gloria and I needed to talk. But I had to go.

The training session that day wasn't really so bad without the printed material. I actually forget how I positioned the naked presentation, but it did work out.

When Gloria and I got the chance to dissect the matter, I was fascinated. Here was a woman of extraordinary intelligence. But here also was a victim, pure and simple. She didn't get that she was accountable. She was more interested in reality. For her, ours was a busy office and realistically things would fall through the cracks. On that morning, and over the day before, they did fall through the cracks. And that was somehow okay because, of course, we were gosh darned busy. And she couldn't be blamed for undercommunicating because, well, Linda was going to be talking to me.

When this little problem occurred, Gloria had only been with us for a short while. It was understandable that she would mismanage things a bit at the start. That was not a problem for me. My issue was with her willingness to deflect to Linda. In later conversations Gloria told me that she was afraid of my being disappointed in her so soon on the job.

"It just came out," she said.

"I understand," I replied.

As months went by, I noticed other signs of defensiveness. Ultimately, Gloria and I started focusing our conversations on victim thinking. Through that process I learned that her parents always thought she should have perfect marks in school because she was so smart. Her father used to get very angry and give her a hard time for not being perfect. He would compare her with her brother who, he said, was not nearly as smart but often did better in school. He called her lazy, and she felt he often held back his love. Over the years Gloria learned to deflect blame and brought this tendency to her job.

Gloria's transformation from victim to agent included a phase in which she had to wrestle with personalization. She discovered that she couldn't just stop behaving like a victim because it meant no longer saying, "It's not my fault." She learned that when she was tempted to say those words, it usually was her fault. But removing that bridge from guilt to defense exposed her to long-felt pain over her father.

We worked together on her self-forgiveness. In one conversation, Gloria asked, "But how can I forgive myself? Many things I set out to do have not been accomplished. I feel like a failure."

Gloria was generalizing and judging herself. The truth was that I was pleased as punch with her work. The goals she set for herself were what we call "realistic stretch goals." Gloria did attain many of her day-to-day goals. But she was not forgiving herself for the ones she missed.

This took us in conversation to the reason that she had adopted a victim orientation in the first place. It was caused by her being habituated to the disappointment her father had in her for never achieving perfection in school. Gloria and I spent time exploring her father's judgments. I had to make it clear that neither I nor she was her father.

Gloria did learn to balance her stretch aspirations with an acceptance of not achieving some of them. She got there by self-forgiveness. She learned about the facts: She had a job. She sometimes identified herself with her job, but she was not her job. It was just a job. The job involved stretch goals. Stretch goals are good because they pull an organization forward. On the job, she was a stretch woman. By definition, some goals could be met and others could not. Gloria was also a family woman. In fact, Gloria's family meant more to her than her job. She knew that I was okay with that. She was okay with that, too. There was no need to be judgmental over her failures, because most of the time she did her absolute best in the context of her job—not her life, but her job.

Gloria was no longer a victim, afraid to own responsibility. She was a true player. She was a cause agent who made big things happen for a living. She didn't spend time on "here's why it's not my fault." Her time was dedicated to "here's what we're doing and how we plan to do it well. Here's what went wrong and here's the plan to avoid it in the future. I am responsible for everything I touch and oversee. Sometimes things don't work out. But I own it. We keep trying and we get better. I don't get hung up on guilt because I'm busy making things work and I trust that I am okay. I have lots to learn."

What a person.

If You Work with a Victim

The first thing you can do is to role-model agency. Don't be a victim yourself of other people's victim thinking!

Typically a victim's lament will fall into one of two categories: Either the issue is over and the victim is looking back and attributing blame, or the issue is unresolved and the victim is positioning himself to be free of culpability.

In the first case, the key is to move the person into a more future-oriented mode. You could ask, "What could you do to avoid a recurrence of the problem?" You may have to ask the question a couple of times. The idea is to shift the victim's attention from blame over a past problem to some aspect of the future, whether related to the problem or not.

In the second case, when the victim is deflecting blame over an unresolved matter, ask, "But what can you do about that?" Typically the reply will be "Nothing." Ask again. "Nothing" will come back at you. Then try, "But if you *could* do something about it, what would it be?" At that point you'll probably get a description of some small role they could play in its resolution.

Repeating these steps with a victim helps the person to relearn how to respond to misfortune.

The above ideas apply even if you manage a victim. But in that circumstance there is yet another guideline to follow. Typically you will find out about some misfortune after it has occurred. You will ask the person about it and you'll hear the victim response. In this case, you can negotiate a new guideline for the victim. Suggest that from then on, when they know something is going awry, you would like them to tell you well in advance of the failure. You can also point out that when they do predict a problem, you would like them to suggest what could be done to preempt the failure.

In all cases, victim behavior can be seen as a reflection of what is going on in the victims' minds. The chatter running through their heads is simply being verbalized; you are hearing how their unconscious minds manage misfortune. Helping people become acquainted with these patterned responses (without labeling) can be profoundly helpful—both to them and to your team.

CHAPTER 6

The Prisoner

I am amazed by how high a percentage of the people who come to me for help say, "I don't know what's bugging me, but I want to get to the bottom of it." It drives them crazy not knowing what's behind their feelings. They feel they are in prison, and they want out.

You would think that somebody who feels troubled would be able to say why. But not being able to pinpoint what is on our minds happens to all of us. We can cite three or four possible causes, but for some reason we can't quite put our finger on the true source of the angst. Sometimes we know the general category of the thing that's bothering us, but we just can't trace the direct link between that heading and the specific anxiety we feel.

We can be prisoners of unresolved arguments, of anger over somebody else's behavior, of guilt over our own behavior. I've worked with parents who lament that their children have grown up and don't need them anymore, leaders who fret over not being able to control a certain employee, employees who groan about feeling trapped in their jobs, and sales managers who "catastrophize" when several sales opportunities in a row have fallen through. Most of these feelings can ultimately be traced to fear, but they manifest themselves at the surface level as highly situation specific.

In one sense, all of us are prisoners, since all of us periodically face challenges that provoke an anxious response. Some people, however, are more troubled by their anxiety than others. These are the ones who seek the help of a coach. They find their reactions either too troubling or too frequent. This chapter is about how these prisoners can break free.

The symptoms of anxiety experienced by prisoners include insomnia, difficulty with concentration, muscle tension, and tightness in the chest. In more serious cases, people complain of sweating, trembling, muscle aches, stomach cramps, and headache. I've also known people who even claim a fear of losing consciousness. When feeling these symptoms, people tend to have elevated pulse and blood pressure. When it comes to working with prisoners of anxiety, the majority of my work is on mild problems caused by the day-to-day challenges of the workplace. I refer people with the more serious problems to medical practitioners.

When people are in prisoner mode, they are less productive. They tend to hide away from managers and fellow workers, avoiding interaction with others. They are preoccupied. They can be snippy in conversation. When flushed out into the open and challenged on any issue, they can be quite volatile. They hurt. Their body language shows defensiveness, and eye contact is less frequent. They are halfhearted, showing up at work for appearance's sake but uninterested until what is bothering them gets sorted out. In a sense, their real work is going on inside.

Prisoners have much in common with worriers. Both are preoccupied while on the job, and both suffer from anxiety. But whereas worriers are concerned about what may happen in the future, prisoners are preoccupied with what has already happened. They have already experienced something that pushed their buttons, and they carry that experience with them.

Prisoners of Anxiety

Prisoners of anxiety are usually wrongly incarcerated. They're behind bars because their unconscious mind is hyperactive. For example, some people tend to catastrophize when bad things happen in their lives. When an unfortunate thing occurs, they blow it out of proportion. In this case, they become prisoners held in what feels like an isolation chamber—totally alone and depressed. Where other people might "feel bad" about the unfortunate thing but quickly move on with their lives, these people feel just terrible and hunker down, endlessly trying to figure out what's wrong.

Take Jay, a client of mine, for example. As a vice president of sales in one of the world's largest high-tech companies, he is the paragon of catastrophizers. If he gets a good report from one of his sales forces, life is good—but only for a few hours. When one little bad thing happens, he fears that it will happen in all parts of his life, for the rest of his life. If sales fall behind the forecast in one month, he assumes the company will go bankrupt. He looks at his kids and worries about their future. How will he send them to college? One little argument with his wife and he begins to think his marriage is falling apart.

Jay knows these responses are not rational, not grounded in reality. In his job, he knows from experience that there will be bad months from time to time. But when they come up, he can't stop himself from panicking.

Another client, Steve, is vice president of acquisitions for a large chain of drugstores. His team's job is to buy eligible independent stores to add to the chain. They target viable enterprises and "seduce" their owners. Then they handhold them through the due-diligence process and the closing of the deal. Every so often Steve's team is ready to take a potential buy to the finish line but the deal is rejected by his boss or a board member. Steve then feels an unusual level of anxiety that lasts for more than a week. "It's overwhelming," he says. "I feel so angry! I'm usually not even involved in the particular deal—but it just pushes my buttons." He may get out of jail when things start going well again, but he knows that, in effect, he's out on day passes: When the next bad thing comes along, it'll be back in the clink for him.

Another example of hypersensitivity is my client Norma's response to the various presentations she must make to her peers. Norma is a divisional president of a major player in the travel industry. She leads an organization of several thousand people. None of them knows of her plight, except for her executive vice president of Human Resources. That person got me involved in helping Norma with her problem.

I learned from our sessions that Norma worries probably a normal amount in advance of a presentation. However, when she's in front of the crowd presenting—that's when the important symptoms of her problem occur. To the audience she sounds confident and clear. But she practically loses consciousness while up there. She trembles. She clenches her buttocks so tightly it practically changes her posture. "My hands shake so much I have to hold onto something to stabilize them," she says.

Like Jay and Steve, Norma knows that her response is uncalled-for. She is a prisoner of anxiety.

Getting to the bottom of Jay's, Steve's, and Norma's hypersensitivity in our coaching sessions involved peeling back protective layers to get to the childhood origins of their anxiety.

■ Jay had to come to grips with the fear of being totally vulnerable. This was a childhood fear he had carried into adulthood.

■ In Steve's case, the reaction to having his department overridden by senior management related to how in childhood his controlling grandmother, who reared him and his siblings, always seemed to step in to stop him from having fun. His grandmother was afraid of being blamed for being too carefree with the kids in her charge. She overcompensated. Steve still carried resentment over her last-minute intrusions into his plans.

■ As for Norma, her oversensitivity was linked to a piano recital when she froze in front of a large audience. She was twelve years old and the trauma affected her deeply.

When big events happen to them, kids automatically make long-term adjustments to their mental programming. Their brains conclude that a certain thing must not be repeated. Whenever something smells like a potential repeat, they react negatively.

It's Often About Childhood

The examples cited so far involve childhood experiences. Just like worriers, prisoners are often dealing with parts of the personality that took shape in childhood to defend against perceived threats. Kids go about their business, exploring and playing, taking for granted that their need for love will be met. If parents consistently make that love appear conditional or unavailable, there will be an inevitable response. The natural construction of an integrated personality is jarred in some way.

■ Joanne was hit as a child. Love was conditional. When she was good, everything was okay. But when she was bad, her basic need for protection was not met. Instead of a hug, it was a cuff to the side of the head. Joanne grew up having to deal with the fear that she would not be loved. Rejection made her anxious.

■ Noah's parents were busy when he was young. He didn't get the attention he craved. Unconsciously he felt he wasn't being loved as much as he wanted to be loved. The result in adulthood was that when his wife became angry with him, he became paralyzed with anxiety until the dispute could be resolved. He couldn't stand his wife being angry because it made him feel the way he felt as a child.

■ Henry's father used to lose his temper. Henry hated the feeling he got when that happened. The flow of love would stop. Now, when Henry's business partner, who tends to have a dominant personality, gets uppity, Henry shrinks away in silence—exactly what he used to do when his father was angry.

■ Wayne's mother had a nervous breakdown when he was very young. Wayne's needs for affection were left to be filled by his father, a busy newspaperman. Wayne felt abandoned, although, of course, he was too young to know the concept. It was just an emptiness he felt a lot of the time. Now, as an adult, when traveling on business, Wayne finds himself feeling anxious. Through coaching he discovered that being away from his home base reminds him of the absolute emptiness he experienced as a child.

Suffering children do not know they are suffering. They just experience life with pain. In most cases, their emotional angst is not processed. It is unfinished business. Because it is unfinished, it recurs in response to circumstances that are interpreted as being similar to the original painful context. It recurs until it is processed.

Of course, not all children are loved as much as they want. It's a fact of life. Even parents who lavish their kids with love can't please them all the time. And if they do choose to please their children all the time, different problems arise: Their kids, not experiencing limits on their behavior and emotions, become spoiled, do not learn to take responsibility, and run other people ragged trying to fulfill their needs. It is a no-win scenario for parents. Maybe Buddhists are right when they say that "life is suffering."

There is a threshold of love needs. If caregivers satisfy enough of those needs, then children grow up to deal with life effectively. They experience anxiety appropriate to the circumstances they find themselves in. At times they hurt, but it is at a level that is somehow appropriate to the circumstances. For example, when they are rejected, they feel the pain of rejection. They cry. But the recovery period is shorter than for prisoners of anxiety.

When caregiving is inadequate, kids grow up wondering why at times they are provoked into anxiety. They notice, for example, that it takes longer for them to recover from emotional upset. Or their anxiety in one area of their life bleeds into other areas. Or they feel guilty for longer than is called for. Or they fear confrontation more than most people do. Or they hold onto anger longer than others. Or they find themselves giving into impulses without the control they wish they had. The list could go on and on.

It's Not Always About Childhood

You don't always have to go back into childhood memories when dealing with anxieties. Indeed, several anxieties are simply about the day-to-day pains of life. They have nothing to do with childhood trauma or poor parenting. For example, hormones and many other brain chemicals can affect mood; when they are out of balance, anxiety might be the result. Medical doctors can address these issues very effectively with prescription medicines.

A midlife crisis is a bit of a prison in and of itself. People can go through years during this time of life with a gnawing feeling of anxiety. "What is my purpose?" "What is my meaning?" and "Why am I here?"—these questions are posed regularly in my practice. They are not just rhetorical pleas for lightning bolts to deliver philosophical satisfaction. They are profoundly honest queries from people who look me straight in the eye as they pose them. They are announcing that they darn well want answers and will feel uncomfortable until they get them.

Other questions about how we will spend our lives can preoccupy us. "Should I have a family?" "I can't have children, so what good am I?" "I feel guilty going back to work after having a child." When anxieties strike over questions like these, there is little value in trying to determine whether the same anxieties were experienced in childhood. They don't usually stem from unresolved childhood issues. Questions about a person's historical family situation may be useful, but revisiting childhood trauma probably is not.

Issues of human mortality often imprison us. When we anticipate or grieve the loss of a loved one, or wrestle with our own fears of death, we can hold onto anguish for a long time. These matters are huge for people. They are not usually about what happened when they were young. They are real, tangible, and painful problems, very much about the present.

So, in coaching sessions, looking into childhood experiences is not always necessary. But it is useful frequently, not because childhood is the source of all angst but because life is angst provoking and we start our lives in childhood! We learn our responses to life's provocations once we get started with life. If we don't resolve or fully process early provocations, then later ones won't be handled very easily. So people seek help. A bad economy, a person's limited job security, a lack of global stability, family stresses—these things jump-start the anxiety. When we have unfinished business from our past, it shows up in these moments.

Getting Out of Jail

Let's assume you feel you are a prisoner of anxiety and have come to me for coaching. How would we proceed?

Isolating the Feeling

The first step is to isolate the feeling and spend some time exploring where it comes from and what its triggers are.

Isolating the feeling is usually pretty easy. We would differentiate it from other things going on in your mind. For example, we would try to see your thoughts about the feeling as separate from the feeling itself. We would determine where in your body the feeling seems to be "located." We would talk about what the feeling "feels like," using whatever words that come to mind for you. You might say it manifests itself as feeling like a pit in your stomach, or a tightness in your chest, or a mild headache. Perhaps you would simply describe it as a gnawing feeling of tension.

Feeling the feeling for a while would allow you to accept it for what it is. Oddly enough, when you experience anxiety, some part of you actually dislikes it so much that you don't really want to go with the feeling. Your brain wants to push it away, but it persists. This struggle to push it away is what must stop in order for you to fully embrace the feeling.

Indeed, the desire to get rid of the anxiety is what keeps it present. As trite as it sounds—and I did think it was trite when I first heard it voiced on television by Sylvester Stallone—"what you resist, persists."

The idea is to locate the feeling in your consciousness and stay with it for a while. I would encourage you, even if it made you curl up and cry, to hold onto it. This alone would help you relieve the anxiety. The struggle for escaping it would be overridden by the willingness to own the anxiety.

Giving the Feeling a Voice

The second step is to give the feeling a voice. I would ask you to "be" the feeling and speak to me. The odds are that you would provide some kind of intellectual answer, and I would have to ask you to stay with the feeling instead. I would seek from you a statement that contains "I feel," followed by an emotion or body sensation. For example, you might say, "I feel scared," or "I am sad," or "I am mad," or "I am empty." I would encourage you to tell me why.

If it sounds as if the feeling could be traced to earlier insecurity or frustration, we would pursue your memories of when you felt that insecurity or frustration in your past. We would explore the similarities between this occasion and that one.

This act of isolating the feeling and exploring its links to your history creates a kind of distance between you and the feeling. You become an observer of the feeling rather than one who is overwhelmed by it. This is very relieving.

Acknowledging the Feeling as Yours

The third step is to acknowledge that the feeling is a part of who you are. It is not something to be avoided like the plague. It is to be accepted and integrated into yourself.

At this point I might ask you to pretend that there is a youngster inside of you who is experiencing this feeling. I would encourage you to visualize putting your arm around that little boy or girl and telling him or her that you will handle the situation that has recently provoked the anxious response.

This accomplishes several things. It provides an anchor for the distancing effect; that is, with an image in your mind of the child, you, the observer of the child, are psychically removed. But you are also nurturing the child, providing the reassurance that he or she has craved all along. The image of placing your arm around the child also creates a context for a long-term relationship between you and the child. You are the adult who will deal with reality and the child is the one who will grow over time under your wing.

Getting Out—and Staying Out

The other important part of coaching a person out of jail is to find practical ways to address the anxiety, should it be triggered again. And so, after you have isolated and held on to the feeling as described above, the next step often is to find the belief that led to the feeling. For example, if you have been feeling guilty about going back to work after having a baby, your underlying belief might be that "women should not go back to work after having a baby." We could question this belief together and assess whether it is acceptable to you. Then, if you changed your belief, the feeling would go away. Later, when the feeling returns, you would know why and apply your rational view on the topic to alleviate the anxiety.

This practice of tracing the current feeling to a specific belief is the foundation of cognitive therapy generally, and rational emotive therapy specifically. It is based on the principle that your interpretation of the world is an equal if not greater contributor to your feelings as, for example, what someone said to you. If you ask most people why they are feeling something, they will attribute it to something that happened in the "outside world," such as "Rick said I did a bad job. He hurt my feelings." This person is not likely to say, "Rick said I did a bad job, and I interpreted it as Rick thinking I am not lovable so I got depressed." However, this latter response is closer to the truth.

The sequence that leads to the anxiety goes like this:

1. An event occurs in the outside world (Rick says I did a bad job).

2. That information travels to my brain.
3. My brain interprets the information (I think, "Rick says I am not lovable").
4. I experience the feeling of rejection.
5. I behave in a certain way (hang my head, feel a tightness in my chest).

The claim that the feeling is caused at least partly by the interpreter, rather than by Rick alone, is based on the fact that other people could be told the same thing by him and not respond in the same way.

So, if our feelings are driven by our interpretations, why do we interpret the way we do? Well, let's resist the temptation to attribute it all to our childhood—though that may be the origin of some of our interpretations. How we interpret situations comes from our beliefs. For example, if we believe that "people who say we did something wrong really believe that we are not lovable," then we will take incoming criticism as a sign of our lack of lovability. But if we believe that "Rick has bad days; that's why he says half the things he says," then we may not have hurt feelings when he criticizes us on a bad day—or maybe even on good days.

Our beliefs come from many sources, including the media, our family, our wider circle of acquaintances, our experiences, and our education. Our beliefs are often formed from generalizations we have heard others make and have made ourselves. For example, we move easily from noticing Robert arriving late for meetings to judging Robert to be a "late kind of guy." And "late kinds of guys" don't really live by their word. And people who don't live by their word shouldn't be trusted. So if you want to rely on a teammate, you can't trust Robert. Our beliefs are often not founded on rational analysis.

It does not have to be a difficult task to unravel these beliefs, so long as you know what you're looking for. The simple question is, what belief causes this reaction? Through dialogue one can uncover that belief and come up with some obvious steps to test its validity. This is when a coaching relationship can be quite brief—consisting of just a meeting and a follow-up phone call.

Maggie was a prisoner of anxiety. She came for coaching because she always felt tense around her coworkers and boss. She was the office manager of a midsize law firm. A large part of her day was spent managing the computer network for the firm. She described her problem as always feeling tense at the office.

"You have no idea how it feels," she told me. "I'm, like, paranoid all the time. The problem is that my boss and most of the other lawyers seem to think I'm hiding something."

I asked her the predictable question: "Are you hiding something?"

"I don't think so," she answered.

"Well, let's assume for a moment that you do have a secret at the office, that there is something you don't want anyone to know. What would it be?"

After a thoughtful pause, she posed her answer like a question and said, "I'm scared? I am afraid people might reject me?"

"Why would they reject you?"

"Well, if people really knew how little I know about the administration of a computer network, then they wouldn't want me in the job anymore."

"That must be frightening. I don't know anything about networks either. Do you ever ask for help?"

"If I asked for help, they would know the truth."

"What happens when things go wrong with the network?"

"I do my best to fix it. But I almost never solve the problem. In fact, when people ask me questions I just bluff it. And the consultants we use are never really available when you need them."

Even when the system was fine, Maggie had anxiety around the possibility that it could crash at any time. So many unexpected crashes occurred that she learned to fear another one "any minute now."

The beliefs underlying her anxiety were twofold. First, she believed that she was not competent in operating a computer network. Second, she also believed that if her boss knew her level of competence, then he would dislike her and maybe fire her. We did not need to explore where her fear of rejection came from (though I suspected it was from her relationship with her father). We just had to find out if it was true that her boss would be upset and likely to let her go.

We talked for a while about what her boss was like and how he and others in the organization appeared to feel about her general level of competence. It turned out that even Maggie suspected that, except for her control of the network, people generally thought pretty highly of her. She had been promoted to office manager because she was an effective team member with strong leadership skills.

"So, Maggie, I think you would be wise to talk to your boss about the network and find out his expectations of you as the person responsible for the network. You might be surprised to find him frustrated not with you but with it."

Maggie agreed to do this. I gave her some pointers on how to approach the topic and get the key questions answered.

She called my voice mail the next day. "I can't thank you enough," she said. "You were absolutely right. He said he felt like I was taking too much responsibility for flaws in a poor software program operating on an old hardware platform. He said he admired my effort to keep us running, and gave me the freedom to find another consulting company to help us fix the network. He asked me to be more open with him so we could work on the problem together. I admitted I was afraid he was going to blame me for the problems. He said he felt guilty dumping the problems on my shoulders." Her relief and excitement were obvious.

This was the end of the coaching project with Maggie. It can be that simple for some people. It depends on things like the intensity of the imprisoning feelings, the self-esteem of the client, the severity of the contributing factors, and the frequency of recurrence. For example, Maggie could have come back with a different story. She could have said her boss was very disappointed in her. She could have reported that even though the conversation went well, she still had the overwhelming fear of exposure and rejection. This would have taken us back to exploring the unresolved feelings from past experiences.

The key to escaping the prison of anxiety is self-awareness. Whether you take the exit of linking current feelings to past feelings, or of exploring the beliefs that underlie your feelings, you end up in a place where you are free to override your automatic emotional responses. Instead of being overwhelmed with angst, you become an observer of an angst response, an observer who is empowered to validate what you see and then move on.

If You Work with a Prisoner

The best thing you can do to support those who have fallen into an anxious response is to help them define what it is that's bothering them. Ask them to tell you their list of possibilities, all the things on their mind that could be contributing to the anxiety. They will probably give you five or six items and claim that none of them really stands out. But almost undoubtedly one of them contains the trigger.

The next logical question is, "Which of these things bugs you the most?" You'll get an answer. Armed with that direction, you can ask what it is about that particular matter that bugs them the most.

Let's look at this in action. You work with a colleague, Bill, who seems to be down in the dumps. You ask why and he says, "I don't know, I guess it's just the stress."

You ask him whether he'd like to talk about it more to figure out exactly what it is. When he agrees, you ask for the list.

"Well, I've got to get the report to John in the next twenty-four hours and I haven't even started it," he says. "And then there's the fact that Lucy wants me to change desks; like I have time to collect all my stuff. Oh, and my phone cord is bugging the heck out me with its stupid static. And then there's this customer complaint that I have to respond to—I resent this being dumped on me."

"What's bugging you the most?" you ask.

After a pause, he comes back with, "It's the desk thing. I am sick and tired of being the nomad around here! Lucy treats me like dirt!"

You're in.

The next thing for you to do is explore what meaning Bill has assigned to whatever communication he has received. Somebody said or wrote something that was interpreted by Bill as evidence that some belief he has is true. Perhaps the belief is that Lucy does not respect him. You could conclude that Bill interpreted Lucy's asking him to move as more evidence of her disrespect. Of course, you know the cold facts contain none of the unspoken line of his thinking. Lucy asked Bill to move. You've got to help Bill stick with the facts.

What you are looking for from Bill is some version of the exclamation "Bingo!" You'll know it when you hear it. It is the sense of relief a prisoner experiences when they move from not knowing what's going on in their head to realizing what it is. That discovery alone will provide some relief.

A guideline for a next step, if one is called for, would be to encourage your friend to stick with the facts. It does not address the more fundamental question about the truth of the belief, but it may provide short-term relief. Alternatively, for final closure, you can encourage ongoing communication.

PART II

Hell Is Not Just Other People

CHAPTER 7

The Transcendence Model

Common explanatory threads have been running throughout the descriptions of the various types we have explored in this book. This chapter reveals that these threads are not random but make up a simple tapestry or model—a powerful model that will help you understand yourself and others around you at work and at home, and help you change in ways you want to change. In fact, this chapter's discussion of the model bears within it the seeds of the rest of the book, which will help you understand the opportunities you have to move beyond fear to freedom in your work and life.

I certainly rely on this model every day. I use it to guide my thinking during conversations with clients. It prompts me to ask myself such questions as:

- What is this person afraid of?

- What does this person not want to face?

- What is this person resisting?

Moving toward answers to these questions helps me understand clients' central challenges. It also helps them gain a broader perspective of what prompted them to come to see me.

A model, according to one definition, is a simplified description of a system to assist with predictions. The accuracy of a model correlates to how useful it is. I would call my model very useful because it does accurately predict people's behavior. Clients see themselves in it.

The Transcendence Model

I call it the Transcendence Model because it explains why we act the way we do and helps us move beyond this behavior, freeing us to be fulfilled and productive. Here it is in its simplest form.

What the Transcendence Model Explains

People are, by nature, very insecure. They spend a great deal of their time seeking security and avoiding more insecurity. These activities give rise to the behavioral tendencies we examined in Part I of this book, such as worrying, seeking to control, and deflecting blame. There is nothing inherently wrong with these and other similar tendencies, unless a person finds them troubling. Spending less time seeking security and avoiding insecurity reduces how often people suffer from feelings of insecurity.

What the Transcendence Model Predicts

The Transcendence Model predicts how individuals will respond to various stimuli and how their behavior will be perceived by other people on the job or at home.

The Transcendence Model as a Tool

Think of the model as a direction pointer. For example, if you wonder why you are behaving a certain way, ask yourself, "How does this apparently problematic behavior manifest my insecurity?" Then you have a sense of direction. The model assumes that everyone who regrets a frequent behavior or has a recurring, unwanted feeling is insecure. To go even deeper, the model prompts the questions, "What am I insecure about?" and "What is the feeling that underlies my insecurity?"

And if you ask yourself, "How can I be less insecure?" the model will suggest that, in addition to addressing the current source of your insecurity, you accept insecurity as part of your humanity. Life is insecure and you are busy avoiding your insecurity.

The model does not come from a single source. It reflects what I have learned through my own reading, my education in philosophy and psychology, my personal therapeutic and meditative experiences, dialogues with colleagues, and, of course, dialogues with clients. In fact, I am positive that I have learned as much from clients as I have from all the other sources combined. Each coaching relationship gives me and the client the opportunity to explore humanity. Not one client has bored me and not one single problem has ever seemed like the "same old thing." Even if the category of problem is repetitive, the circumstances are always different. And one person's pain is unique to that one person.

Nor has the model been tested in an academic or scientific fashion, though certain aspects of it have gained some degree of academic credibility. For example, cognitive therapy is an accepted therapeutic model that says people can deal with their psychological problems by understanding the thoughts and beliefs underlying their moods and behaviors. Principles of this accepted thinking have made it into my coaching methods and into this book.

What I know for sure is that the model has worked very effectively as a tool to guide me through my coaching conversations and to help my clients make great progress.

You know how sometimes it's a simple thought or question that unlocks a task? Let's say, for example, that you have to give a big presentation and you don't know how to organize your thoughts. So you ask an experienced presenter for some advice. That person says, "Well, keep in mind that the audience members are always asking themselves, 'What's in this for me?' If you organize your thoughts around answering that question, then you've won half the battle." Suddenly you have a place from which to begin your preparations.

In the same way, the Transcendence Model helps you sort out what is going on in your mind when something is bothering you. It is a tool to get you started in understanding the various types of people with whom you work. The model is meant to be a tool to help you begin and to make progress when you are stuck.

Once you get started, you might veer away from the model. That's okay. The principles described here are too simple to represent the entirety of what you are wrestling with. The model will not answer all of your questions but it will point you in a fruitful direction. It has never failed me as a coach and as a person who has had his own struggles with things like worrying, seeking to control, and desiring the notice of others.

Consider a man named Edward who came to me because he wasn't sure whether he should stay in his job or not. He explained that he questioned himself on a daily basis. He said that he had left a great job for his current role as a vice president of marketing for a medium-size chain of hardware stores. The problem was that he was working for an "egocentric control freak," as he put it. Should he change again? Should he put up with his boss? These were his presenting questions.

Edward and I explored how his boss made him feel. The model told us to go there. His answer was that his boss made him feel "small." His style was invalidating. Through further coaching sessions, Edward concluded that his sense of self-worth was too dependent on the esteem others had for him. The model took us there. Fine. But he left the job anyway because he found it unfulfilling. In other words, the model helped him find out what was pushing his buttons, but it also directed his attention to questions about what he really wanted. It could not predict that he was bored. That was something he discovered just by shining a light on the whole array of issues facing him.

The model takes people to deeper psychological and existential realities. You may ask, "Why do I need to explore my deepest fears if I am simply trying to be a less controlling person?" Or, "Why does overcoming worry mean that I have to think of when I felt insecure as a child? Isn't coaching about survival tips rather than a therapeutic foray into anguish?" My answer to these questions is that survival tips don't usually work in the long run. They are like carbohydrates, initially satisfying but quickly burned off. The goal of understanding ourselves requires going further than tips can take you. It requires transcending your personal paradigm in order to see yourself in a new, perhaps broader perspective, sparking more informed choices.

Love, Death, and Robots

So far in this book, by analyzing the six types of businesspeople, we have exposed some key components of the model. One central point is that all through our lives we are very much in need of love and affection. The need is built right into the species because it affects our chances for long-term survival. If the species effectively provides security for its young, then it is healthy. If it does not, then it is at risk of demise.

Often we are not satisfied in our quest for affection. In that sense, many children are on tenterhooks. They are vulnerable to swings in the amount of attention and affection they receive. If affection is conditional, then a pattern of aiming to please sets in. If the effort to please fails, then the child might experience anger as a result. If the effort to please sometimes succeeds and sometimes fails, then concern over getting control of the source of security sets in. We worry about being secure and we work hard at guaranteeing our security.

Also touched on through the exploration of the types is that when we accept this insecurity about our lives, we are less at battle. This is counterintuitive, of course, because we are already attempting to avoid battles within and without by avoiding insecurity. But we are so busy in our avoidance that we become obsessed in one way or another.

- The worrier is obsessed with thoughts about what needs to be avoided.

- The controller is obsessed with maintaining a state of security.

- The fake is hiding from insecurity.

- The attention-seeker is compensating for insecurity.

- The victim is defending against insecurity.

- The prisoner is wrestling with the insecurity that has invaded his consciousness.

Whatever form it takes, this obsession operates on the illusion that insecurity is not a necessary condition, that it can be avoided. But we can't avoid it. At least, we can't seem to avoid it in most cultural scenarios. Insecurity is, in this sense, the name of the game. Yet we fight it.

There are other reasons we can't beat insecurity. In a sense, it is a part of nature. We are, after all, going to die. That tends to evoke insecurity. Right off the bat there is a need built right into our value system. We need to live forever because, presumably, death is the end of what we love. Life is the name of the game. Death is the loss of the game. We must die. So we must be losers. We fight so hard not to lose!

We are also insecure because our feeling of self, of being distinct entities, cuts us off from the whole. So often I have looked at a mountain range and bemoaned my inability to be one with it. My individuality cuts me off from my participation in a oneness. Again, insecurity is the name of the game.

The model suggests that we can embrace this fact of life. We can own our humanity. We can accept our insecurity—that we are not likely to ever feel full forever, that we will die, that not all our goals can be met, that we can't quite merge with the universe because of our separateness. The suggestion is that if we accept ourselves for what we are, then we are no longer struggling against the facts of life. We can find peace. In fact, if we stop spending our mental energy addressing insecurity, we can come face-to-face with the possibility of fulfillment in the present.

However, reducing how hard we work at insecurity does not mean, for instance, that we become less capitalistic or that we lose our core motivation. It means that we are not so robotically inclined to do what we do. As a matter of fact, it opens us to the possibility of choice. We can choose to work like crazy people or to become like the laziest of people— it's our choice.

Owning our humanity partly means realizing that much of what we do is a reflection of how we are programmed to fill the gaps of insecurity. When they are engaged in their defining behaviors, the worrier, the controller, the fake, the attention-seeker, the victim, and the prisoner are engaged like automatons in seeking security and avoiding insecurity. These people know that the behavior is not something they do with conscious purpose (though there is unconscious purpose). That is why they sought help in the first place. This programming has the noblest intention of helping us find the nourishment we need for a healthy species. But it also robs us of the capacity to operate at a higher level. Instead of sidestepping our robotic impulses, we are trapped in them.

Rising Above

The good news is that we can transcend our angst and find a kind of freedom. Rising above means not just accepting our humanity but also making choices in our lives that go against our basic programming to satisfy ourselves. For example, recall that Joyce the worrier learned to do the opposite of what she wanted in order to rise above her program of giving in to her impulses. My advice to her was: "If you want ice cream now, wait fifteen minutes. If you want to take the escalator, then take the stairs." By learning to self-override, we learn to rise above the habitual programs designed by our nervous system to seek out security and avoid insecurity.

When we gain awareness of our basic programming, we are suddenly empowered to choose otherwise and we open a door to self-fulfillment. This is a beautiful thing. If you tend to control people and you realize that it's a response to the belief that being out of control means putting your sense of security in jeopardy, you gradually learn how this program affects you on a moment-by-moment basis. As that self-awareness builds, so, too, does the capacity to choose otherwise. That, to me, is humanity at its best. We are not just robots. We get to choose. Awareness of how and why we tend to behave robotically empowers us, challenges us, to rise above and begin to make choices.

When we behave like robots, we don't see the options. We assume that we just behave that way. In fact, we assume that there is no other way to behave. We then suffer from the illusion that we *are* the programming. We identify ourselves with the programming. And when we emote about our current status of security, we have the illusion that we are that emotion. We become identified with that emotion.

But when we suddenly become aware of how the emotion is merely the result of our programmed effort to act or not act, we disidentify from the illusion. We have become the observer rather than the thing being observed. We are suddenly able to say, "I have this emotion, but I am not this emotion." That, too, is a beautiful thing.

First Principles

The explanations and insights of this chapter are not dependent on laboratory research or psychological field testing. They can be derived just from thinking about them. They are accessible from thought. They are *a priori*, as philosophers would put it: not dependent on experience. Let's see how this is so by going on a little mind trip together.

First, let's get ready. Set aside thoughts about your friends and loved ones and all of your responsibilities. Think of yourself simply as a consciousness. You are awake. But, for this thought experiment, assume you know nothing. There is nothing you are thinking of. The lights are on, but nobody's home. Let's go so far as to say you don't even know that you are human. You can think, but that's about all. At this point you have no sense of "I." Everything seems as a dream and you don't know what is real. It's as if you have a serious case of amnesia. You are going to try to figure out what is going on. And you want to be very sure that what you conclude is not a dream.

The philosopher Descartes asked, "What can I know for sure?" He came up with the dictum "I think, therefore I am." You say to yourself, "Okay, I don't know what's going on. I don't even know what is true. But I do know I'm thinking, so one thing is for sure. I exist. I know that because somebody in here is doing the thinking."

So, from nothingness we can agree, "I exist." Now let's build on that by introducing the notion of time. Once you accept that you exist, you discover that you want to continue to exist. Living things, from amebas to zebras, seek to live. With continued existence in mind, we suddenly have wants and needs.

We turn now to psychologist Abraham Maslow's "hierarchy of needs" for a contribution to our logic. The desire to live introduces you to physiological needs that you very much want fulfilled. As Maslow would put it, you first want to fulfill your needs for food, water, and air because these are necessary for life. Notice that we have now established your existence and your wants. And that sets up the problem.

You discover that there are other people out there. They, too, are in this thought experiment. They are sometimes in the way of your satisfying your wants and needs. As the French philosopher Jean-Paul Sartre suggested, "Hell is other people." Without much time going by, you know they are there because you bump into them as they deny you what you want from life.

So now we have you, your needs, and other people. You have to get along with the other people in order to get what you need. Unless you are stronger than everyone else, in which case you can just clobber them and steal what you want, some form of cooperation is called for. But that's not all. You also don't want to bully them because it turns out, according to Maslow, that in addition to your physiological needs, you also want their company. Babies are born this way. It makes sense, when you think about it. If babies—even the offspring of wild animals—didn't seek the security of at least their mothers, then they would not survive. They could be killed by predators or they might just not get the nourishment they need for life.

You spend your life trying to get this security and trying to avoid insecurity. Along the way, things make you angry. Sometimes you read signals that tell you that you might not get what you want, so you feel worried. Or you seek the attention of others in order to feel secure. At other times you infer that they will only give you what you want if you satisfy certain conditions, so you adopt a habituated role to project the right image. Sometimes things go wrong for you. Rather than risk taking the blame in their eyes, you resist that blame and deflect it elsewhere. What else can you do? If you take the blame, it might result in more insecurity.

You have to be pretty quick on your feet to survive in this world. You can't be waiting for proof of things all the time, so you generalize. When one person does a certain thing that hurts you, and then someone else does the same thing, you can't afford the continuation of that thing. So you conclude, very quickly, that everybody is going to do that thing and you had better avoid that thing. In fact, you discover that generalizations serve you well, so you become well practiced at them.

To make sure your security is in good shape, you go around the place asking yourself, "Are things the way I think they need to be?" If they are not, you judge them as unacceptable, potentially harmful to your security. If they are the way they need to be, then things are fine. This constant questioning serves you well and it becomes the foundation of a tendency to make value judgments—very handy.

So far we have established a clear pattern in your behavior. In certain moments you judge, or you experience angst, or you fear. In longer snippets of time these things translate into other behaviors: In order to optimize your sense of security, you blame (victim), or you fret over the future (worrier), or you order people around a lot of the time (controller), or you hide (fake), or you constantly need to be noticed (attention-seeker), or you are bound by anxiety over something in the past (prisoner). Each of the problematic types discussed in this book can be traced to the tendency to judge, to experience angst, and to blame. All the people discussed are robotically programmed to engage in these behaviors in response to perceived threats and opportunities concerning security.

A Better Way

But there is another option available to us. It has profound implications concerning human happiness and productivity. It is possible, through awareness of these motivations, to make different choices. Instead of judging, you can be nonjudgmental. This would reap huge rewards for you. Others would feel more validated and you would experience less fear, anxiety, and frustration. Instead of getting lost in your angst, you can embrace it as part of your reality. This would alleviate stress, reduce the struggle to fight it and compensate for it, and thereby buy time and contentment. Instead of being fearful, you can relax your need to control, be less blame oriented, and worry less.

This is not hypothetical. People who work at the problems we have been discussing end up experiencing the benefits just described. At a personal level they report a greater sense of empowerment. They are less riddled by negative emotions. They have improved relationships. They are flagged as being of high value in their organizations. They generally go further in their careers.

In a sense, these changes make a person more down to earth. Rather than generalizing, you can stay focused on the facts. Rather than blaming, you can focus on the present and the future. Rather than hiding your vulnerability, you can expose it, knowing that facts are facts and you are okay with the facts about you. You have nothing to hide. Rather than seeking attention, you can seek task fulfillment and personal fulfillment in the process. Rather than seeking control because of the false sense of satisfaction that it offers, you can get more done by empowering others. More broadly, rather than attending to how facts can be interpreted based on their possible impact on your security, you can just focus on the facts.

Going Meta

Let's talk more about what it means to "stay with the facts."

Think of the world as being made up of things—this dog over here, that telephone over there, Mexico down there, this rock at my feet. The existence of these things is usually not in question. The fact is, they are objects in the world and probably no one but an ivory-tower philosopher is going to dispute their existence. The world is full of objects.

In my head is a representation of those objects (the objects themselves are not in my head, of course—my brain has created its own picture of them and that picture is in my consciousness). We are going to call thoughts about the real things in the world, the facts in the world—facts like "Jimmy is taller than Belinda"—"object-level" thoughts. If I think "this report is late," that is an object-level thought. It is a fact that the report is late.

We need, for our purposes in this book, to distinguish between object-level thoughts—thoughts about the facts of the world—and opinions about the object-level. We highlight this difference in order to make the point that it's the opinion level that causes us the problems. The name we'll give to this opinion level is "meta-level." We say "meta" because opinions about things are kind of one level higher than the things themselves ("meta" is a prefix meaning "beyond" or "of a higher order").

The meta-level concerns the meaning we apply to the object-level. The report may be late, but in my opinion, over and above that fact, the late report is just one more late thing from this employee, and it's driving me crazy. The opinion is the meaning I am applying to the lateness of the report.

There is nothing inherently wrong with the meta-level. It serves us well. It gives us beauty. While a mountain is just a mountain, when I look at a mountain I import into my experience my meta-level thoughts about its beauty. The meta-level also concerns morality. If someone says an untruthful thing, they just said what they said. The meaning we import about the matter—that saying untruthful things is wrong—that comes from meta-level activity. Meaning gives us, well, meaning. Dogs don't celebrate poetry. Humans do. Kitty cats don't take on a mission to keep peace in the world. Humans do. Bumblebees are busy—you could even say they even have a purpose about them—but they are not aware of their purpose. They are just fulfilling. They operate at the object-level. Humans operate at the object-level and are motivated at the meta-level. They have purpose.

Meta-level thoughts and statements are about object-level things. They address the desirability or undesirability of things. They also refer to truth or falsity, goodness or badness, acceptance or rejection. They produce meaning. That meaning drives us forward in the most profound way. From meaning we see religion, spirituality, purpose, value. We see self.

However, like everything in the world, there is a darker element to the meta-level. The types of people described in this book have problems that come right out of meta-level thinking. Meaning is crucially important. It takes a fair bit of security or self-esteem to resist the temptation to run with meaning in ways that affect us negatively. If your boss says there are layoffs coming, it's hard to take that statement and stop there. No, the possibility of layoffs reflects on your future security and that merits some attention, right? Well, we're not talking about dispensing with meaning. But it needs to be managed.

Some of our meta-level thoughts get some of us into trouble. The Transcendence Model helps people whose meta-level thoughts lead them to periodically undesirable feelings and behavior. For example, worriers take the facts, extend them into a possible future, and create a new possible meaning at the meta-level. "If I lose my job, I won't be able to pay my mortgage!" is not an object-level concern. The mortgage is at the object-level. The pink slip is at the object-level. The phone ringing when the bank doesn't get the payment is at the object-level. But the scary thoughts are at the meta-level. They are based on meaning. We've seen this in light of the worrier. Now think of the other five types:

■ *Controllers* create meaning out of what they perceive to be out of control. A project may be going this way and that, at the object-level, and the controller brings in the meta-level perspective that things are out of control. "Out of control situations are undesirable," he thinks to himself. He steps in to "fix it."

■ The *fake* creates and operates on meaning when she fabricates and projects an image for others to see. She is not just randomly picking an image for us. She prefers the chosen image. To her, it is good. And if she frets over the difference between what she believes or feels versus the chosen image, it is because somewhere in her head she has made the judgment about the hypocrisy. It is bad.

■ When the *attention-seeker* feels lack of the affection he so craves, he is operating on the meta-level belief that he is not okay without attention. He waves his flag out of meta-level discomfort. He seeks meaning through being noticed by others.

■ *Victims* create meaning by thinking about and attributing blame. Rather than staying at the object-level and dealing with the facts, they create a whole new world out of meaning. Their meta-level attention introduces blame. There is no actual blame in the world, of course. You can't touch blame. Oh, you can show a cause-and-effect relationship between two events, but you can't, at the object-level, show how the value judgment implicit in blame is justified.

■ *Prisoners* get locked away by associations they make between their object-level perceptions and their meta-level beliefs and feelings. They import meaning to circumstances that they later regret importing.

The experience of self is at the meta-level. It's one of the intangible things. Self is not an object in the world. You can't touch a self. You can touch a person physically but there is no direct access to the self. Self is an intangible judge of objects, a subject to which we now turn in more detail.

CHAPTER 8

Here Comes the Judge

There are times when you want to reduce the frequency or intensity of certain experiences. You may want release from the nuisance of certain obsessive thoughts or compulsive behaviors, whether you are a worrier, fake, victim, or any of the other types we have discussed. To make these moves, you will need to rise above—to transcend—the paradigm of security and insecurity. For example, instead of running with the victim's temptation to hold onto external blame, you can realize that blaming is a manifestation of your own insecurity. Or instead of trying so hard to draw attention to yourself, you can know that you are okay as you are.

To clarify how this could work for you, we have differentiated your understanding of the facts from your opinions of those facts. We labeled those two things "object-level" thoughts and "meta-level" thoughts, respectively. The behaviors that define the types explored in this book come from meta-level thinking. They are meta-level responses to object-level thoughts. In one way or another, the responses are the result of people's aversion to insecurity. Presumably they are intended to move us toward security, though perversely they usually have the opposite effect.

Do We Need the Meta-Level?

So why not just turn off meta-level thoughts altogether? Surely that would stop the undesirable elements, wouldn't it?

Unfortunately, it wouldn't be sensible to somehow disable the meta-level aspect of our consciousness. The meta-level activities bring us great benefit: meaning, purpose, beauty, goodness, value. No, even if we could do so, turning off meta-level thinking would be undesirable.

Turning off meta-level activity would also deny us our emotions. Even though there are plenty of people—we call them "cold" or "insensitive"—who think emotions serve little purpose, there is ample reason to dispense with that line of thinking. Aside from passion and intensity—things that in themselves are critical aspects of our humanity—emotions play a necessary role in our thinking and living. They help us to set goals, establish our values, and intuit what we think is right for us. They inform us about nurturing our young. Rather than dispense with emotionality, the challenge is to manage certain emotional responses so that we are able to use our emotions rather than simply becoming them. Meta-level thinking can be a key rather than a jail. But the key can only be used by each of us, individually.

In this chapter we're going to look at the self and its judging activities: judgments that keep you bound to old habits and behavior and judgments that free you from these habits and behavior. By the end of the chapter, you will begin to see a clear distinction between having a sense of self that is trapped in the meta-world and an experience of self that is grounded in the object-level world.

Making Judgments

Your positive and negative emotions come from judgments you make of the object-level world. For example, assume that you are at your desk going about your business when you receive a message from a colleague with whom you frequently experience tension. You detect in the message, just in the way it is worded, that the person is once again getting snarky. Perhaps it is a certain subtle jab that really pushes your buttons. The message says, "I am concerned about various alignment issues that might arise between your department's implementation of its new policies versus what has been set out in the senior management team's recent directive."

Of course, somebody else might not detect any problem with the words that have been chosen. They tell you, "Lighten up. He means just what he says." But you believe there is a game being played all the same. You say to your friend, "I don't think so. This guy has an ego the size of a house. For heaven's sake, look at how he positions himself—it's like he's the watchdog for the executive team! Who does he think he is?"

You find yourself offended. You see the object-level words but you reach a lot of meta-level opinions. It happens to everybody. You move from the facts to the judgment. "This guy is a real doofus," you think. Your emotions are firing. The meta-level has done its deed.

Examples abound. The news gets out that a competitor is laying off employees and suddenly your organization is filled with fear. Newspapers report the breakout of an infectious disease in a city, and suddenly all people flying in from that city are suspect. A photocopier breaks down three days in a row, and you find yourself being wary of everything that its manufacturer produces. When a junior colleague who has made two mistakes in one week shows up late on the following Monday, you shake your head and think, "I may have a problem here."

If you want to manage your emotional tendencies, you will need to manage your meta-level thinking. The tendencies to worry, control, fake it, seek attention, attribute blame, and get all wound up in the past are all the results of emotionally driven, meta-level-created judgments.

Who Is the Judge?

To come to this clearer idea of how to rise above the behavior bothering us, we need to explore the notion of self. We want to know exactly who this judge is. Armed with this understanding, we will be able to figure out how to manage the programmed responses we fall into.

One way to approach the subject is to consider what it would be like to have no self. The American psychologist Julian Jaynes, in his book *The Origin of Consciousness in the Breakdown of the Bicameral Mind*, describes what it would be like to be a person from ancient times, before the self evolved as part of humanity. Following his lead, let's try to imagine being without a sense of self. Picture yourself driving a car. Of course, as an experienced driver, you usually end up thinking about other things while you're driving. The car seems to drive by itself. Somehow your background consciousness does the work. For example, driving along, seeing a stoplight, putting your foot on the brake, waiting for the green light, looking both ways, proceeding through the intersection—you do these things unconsciously while your thoughts are elsewhere. Now here's the key: If you subtract those elsewhere thoughts, you have what life would be like without a self. Just observing the objects of the world and responding to them. Self, it could be said, is an add-on.

What in fact is happening in such situations? The meta-level you is busy chattering away to itself while the object-level you deals with the driving. You are the person driving the car while the self is the one with all the thoughts.

Now imagine just driving! No chatter in your head. Imagine just walking somewhere and being aware of the walking without any worry, or tightness, or craving for affection. Some would say this is the goal of Buddhist meditation: to be attentive to the here and now. Others would suggest that this would be optimal human experience, perhaps the stuff of self-actualization. Still others would suggest that this is the way to play a good game of golf. It requires that the sense of self be set aside while the rest of you is engrossed in the present.

How wonderful it would be to stay at the object-level when we want to! We would set the stage to be free of hurt feelings, worry, a sense of insecurity, the anxious need to control. We could look to action plans to address problems rather than looking backwards to place blame or hold on to our regrets. To gain this versatility, we could learn to see ourselves more realistically. We could invest just a little bit more selectivity in our thoughts. We could resist the temptation to go from facts to judgments.

The Experience of Self

Meta-level thinking also gives us the experience of self. The object-level fact that we exist at least as bodies walking around the planet cannot be denied. But the actual experience of self, a volitional, distinct entity who is somehow inside the body, but who feels that regardless of what the body is up to (at least until the body dies), this self exists—that is a meta-level experience.

You can't touch, see, or perceive in any other way somebody's self or sense of self. Even scans of the brain tell us the experience of self does not occur in a specific area of the brain; apparently there are many areas of the brain that periodically participate in producing the experience. So we don't know where your experience of self comes from. As a matter of fact, we don't even know for sure that you have one. Western scientists veered away from the study of something so inaccessible decades ago.

Yet most of us are sure we personally have a sense of self. When we wake up in the morning, we feel like the same person we were the day before. We use the word *I* as though the word has some referent in the real world. We blur the line between the world of objects and the meta-level world of meaning. We each operate as though there were an object of some sort in the world called our personal "self," but when we actually go to grab that object it slips from our fingers.

Self is a meta-level production: You construct your sense of self. You don't do it on purpose, as in, "Today I'm going to adopt this particular persona." You do it automatically, as in, "I am this, and that, and that. I look like this and I speak like this. I think like this. I have this history. This is who I am: this person with all these tendencies." All your object-level thoughts about yourself lead to a singularity.

As a matter of fact, your experience of self can change as the moments of the day pass. Consciousness seems to take on the form of what crosses its path. You can be a cool cat walking alone down your street in sandals, shorts, and sunglasses one day, and an engaged listener nodding and empathizing with a friend on the next. "I am a cool cat," you say on the first day, and "I am a good listener" on the next. You slide right into these roles, taking yourself very seriously.

Lighten Up!

To be less of a worrier, controller, fake, or any of the other problematic types, you would be smart to take yourself a little less seriously. It's not easy to do, of course, but that's probably what people have been telling you when you have been engaged in your troublesome behavior.

"Lighten up!" they say.

And you say back, "That's easier said than done. This is who I am."

It's hard to pick yourself up by your own bootstraps, isn't it? You, your self, when you are feeling some kind of angst, in some strange way, become the angst. You even rely on the verb *to be* in order to communicate your angst. You say, "I am angry." It's like saying, "I am the embodiment of anger itself!" You can't just switch it off. After all, if you are the angst, who is left to flick the switch? It would call for some kind of transcendence. But transcendence is exactly what we are talking about.

It reminds me of a recurring problem I experienced during the days when I did a lot of public speaking. I would stand in front of groups of people and confidently declare, "You can choose to be happy! When you're down, don't be! Pick yourself up." I would look very intense during these moments. My eyes would squint with certainty. My voice would be loud and clear. I knew that the volume of my voice and the absolute certainty of the message would tend to elevate the audience.

Then, after the event, I would get into a car or go up to my hotel room. In a private, reflective moment, relaxing and thinking about the presentation a bit, my thoughts would settle and I would find myself admitting, "I don't buy it." But the next day I would get up and tell the same "lie" to another group.

The reason I thought it was a lie is that I was really never able to do it myself. I couldn't cheer myself up when I was down. In fact, when my wife would see me moping around a bit, and she was in a certain mood, she would say to me, "Okay smarty pants, go ahead—make yourself happy. Be a little Shirley Temple for me. 'Pick yourself up and dust yourself off!'"

Should we take all of our emotional responses less seriously? Well, many times the answer is a flat-out no. As we have said, feelings are critical. They are a response to the world and their purpose is to keep us behaving in a way that helps the species to thrive. Feelings lead us to make babies. They make us cherish life. They inform our every decision. When they are negative or painful, we are best to embrace them to move through them.

But if you are consistently engaged by some matter and you conclude that the anxiety or intensity is not a desirable or useful response, then lightening up might be smart. But here's the tricky thing. Because we identify with our feelings, it is difficult for us to gain any distance from them. To learn how to do this, we need to think a bit more about how we manufacture self.

Where Self Comes From

When you look at a cup, your brain creates a representation of that cup in order for it to enter your consciousness. As we have discussed, the cup in your head is at the object-level. In fact, the information being transmitted to the brain is much more than will ultimately enter into consciousness. Consciousness does not have the bandwidth to accommodate all of the real-world data pertaining to the cup and its position on the table. The brain binds relevant data and sends the bound image to your consciousness. I believe scientists have established this much to their mutual satisfaction. The brain creates a singularity out of the diverse data bits from which it gets to choose. As the British biologist Richard Dawkins puts it, "Maybe [self] consciousness arises when the brain's simulation of the world becomes so complete that it creates a model of itself."

Of course we don't really know for sure where self comes from. That's one problem with the meta-world. It posits the existence of things that can't be touched or proven. The meta-level specializes in things that are over and above the facts of the world. In our case, at the object-level we have our bodies, our activities, our histories, our connections with other people and things. The binding of all of these aspects of our lives into a singularity is a meta-level creation. As such, self is evanescent. Our identity is never as fixed as we think it should be.

For example, many people experience what some refer to as a spiritual crisis. When someone goes through such a period, he asks himself things like, "Who am I?" and "What is my meaning?" I believe these questions flow very logically from our experience of self. Such a person at once has the visceral experience of "I exist," or, "I am," and the logical questions that flow from that experience—"But what am I?" and "Why am I?"—is what they're asking.

These questions are not to be treated lightly. As a coach I help people who are facing such crises of meaning to first experience the loneliness of the questions. People slowly need to embrace the possibility of there being no external, object-level answer to the question, "Who am I?" other than "Whoever I want to be." The question, "What is my meaning?" is answered, after some terror over the fact there is nothing forthcoming, with, "Whatever I take on as my meaning." Initially people hope there is some externally assigned answer. But there isn't. There is personal choice.

Our sense of self, when it is independent of the object-level, is pretty much limited to the judgments that cross its mind. These can be positive judgments, as in, "What a lovely sunset!" Or they can be negative ones, as in, "That man is evil!" But when the sense of self is grounded in object-level thoughts, we have more down-to-earth reactions like, "Sitting at my computer, reading this message, John is asking for help."

There is no sense of independent "I" in this statement. It is a peaceful, nonjudgmental experience of the object-level. There is no sense of a self, busy making value judgments or moving to defend itself or commence an attack—there is no ego.

Ego

The word *ego*, from the Latin word for *I*, has several meanings and uses. We are going to use the word with a very specific meaning in mind.

That meaning is not Freud's. He said ego was the conscious self, the part that interacts with the world and manages other impulses. Nor is it what others refer to as the "false self." The idea here is that when we were kids, sometimes our normal needs for attention and affection coincided with times when our parents were preoccupied with their own struggles and anxieties. As British psychoanalyst D. W. Winnicott says, at these times we "impose a coherence on ourselves"—a false self. This false self survives the anxious times by complying with parental direction while masking a healthy unfolding of individuality. Nor are we using the word *ego* as people commonly do when referring to an exaggerated sense of self-importance, as in "Rupert's ego is as big as all outdoors," or "His ego came into it, and he lost his temper."

Following the Transcendence Model discussed in the previous chapter, we will refer to ego instead as the part of the personality that seeks security and responds to threats against security. Let's look at this in the light of the six types:

- When you are worried, you are afraid for your security. Your ego is active.

- When you're angry because you're not in control, you perceive a threat to what you think will make you secure. Your ego is engaged.

- When you are faking it, you are hiding some truth about yourself out of a feeling of insecurity. This is an ego-managed phenomenon.

- When you seek attention, you seek the feeling of security that gaining it offers. Attention-seeking is ego.

- When you are behaving like a victim, you reveal an insecurity about taking responsibility. The ego deflects responsibility, if that's the name of its game.

- When you feel like a prisoner of your emotions, you feel insecure and you want to get to the bottom of it. Ego drives the inquiry.

The six types discussed in this book all reflect ego. The ego is busy trying to find and sustain optimal security.

Ego and self-esteem are two poles of the *self* dimension. When there's lots of self-esteem, there is low ego, and vice versa. When I feel able and worthy, my ego is not as likely to become engaged. After all, it already feels secure in itself. When I have low self-esteem, my ego has a full-time job ahead of it.

By now a pattern may be emerging for you:

- Your meta-level thoughts generate opinions about your object-level world.

- You are born with the tendency to have these meta-level thoughts because they allow you to survive in the world. They are busy judging what you see. They lead to your emotional responses.

- Your sense of self also comes from these meta-level thoughts insofar as your ability to reach these conclusions happens to give you the ability to create a singularity about yourself.

- When you judge, you become your judgments. When you judge that you are insecure, your sense of self, in the form of ego, acts to defend in some way.

It is interesting that when you judge others, you end up strengthening your sense of self. When you can say, "Ferdinand is a bad man," you are essentially stroking your own ego in the process. You are basically saying, "I am able to judge Ferdinand, and I judge him to be bad. Being capable of making this judgment means that I at least know what bad is." The judgment has strengthened you. Your sense of self is now somehow bigger and stronger.

In this sense, the answer to the question, "Who am I?" is, "I am the judge." The irony is that to become less of one of the six types described in this book, you must reduce the frequency of your judgments of others and of yourself. The more you judge, the further you get from taking yourself less seriously. The more you judge, the more your emotions become engaged. You are the judge. You are the problem. We need less of you. To make the changes you seek, you need more object-level participation in your world and less judgment.

Self as an Illusion

Most of us think we are something special. But let's face it, this planet is populated by millions of species all having evolved from the original activity of a bunch of amino acids long, long ago. I—Art Horn—mean very little in the big scheme of things. Yet I walk around the planet with some sense of self-importance.

We humans in the Western Hemisphere tend to celebrate the self. But when you think of the vast number of species on this planet, and the number of solar systems in this galaxy, and the number of galaxies in this universe, and the possible number of dimensions in the world, well glorioski! When I walk down the street, strutting my stuff, well, how foolish I am! The diversity of the world is too vast to place much value on the relevance of one member of that diversity.

Self-importance is a bit of an illusion. But that's not all. For all I know, self itself may be an illusion. I don't propose you reach the same conclusion yourself—this book doesn't depend on your reaching the same conclusion—but it does happen to be my suspicion.

Certainly the *feeling* of self as an actual entity in the world, independent of body, may be an illusion. We accept that the body is not an illusion. It is part of the world of objects. But because the experience of self is a fabrication of the meta-level, what is its status?

Does beauty exist? Do right and wrong exist? They are things we refer to, but they are constructs, things built in the mind. Does a poem exist before it is spoken or written? I think not. But I can't be sure. I guess it depends on what we mean by "exist."

Most scientists and philosophers have historically bypassed the problem of self altogether. They only spend time on things that can be objectively measured. They neither accept nor reject self as an existing thing. Generally, "not interested." That's a smart move. Very safe.

Buddhists suggest that self is an illusion. That it doesn't really exist. During Buddhist meditation, one experiences mindfulness of the present. In a sense, during this state, the sense of self as a separate entity is lost. Instead, one is immersed in what one is doing, what we called earlier the "real world." In this state we operate at the object-level. The meta-level is no longer actively positing the existence of self as an entity separate from the rest of the world.

This feeling of separateness that Buddhists shed may indeed be an illusion possessed by the rest of us. If it is an illusion, it may be a necessary one in the corporate world or the Western economy. Differentiation, after all, is the name of the game. My advice is, don't sell your worldly goods until you've got your permanent residency status in Tibet.

For now, just know that we have a brain that creates a singularity out of what it perceives. When it applies this binding capacity to its own functioning, it creates the feeling of self. When it attends to the objects of the world, without judging them, it can experience simplicity and connectedness. When it judges—which it must do in order to survive—it enters dangerous territory. It identifies with its own opinions. It creates meaning and galvanizes emotional responses. When it feels empty or challenged, it responds as ego. It can think it is very special and get hung up on this belief.

Without the full experience of the present, we crave substance; we fear our insubstantiality.

The Challenge

I had a conversation about all of this with a client not long ago and he challenged me to apply these notions to myself. He asked me several questions. Here is how the dialogue went.

"So, who are you?" he asked.

"Well, when I am just working in my garden, I am nobody. I am immersed in the garden."

"And when you are coaching?"

"I am for the person I coach. I don't really have a predominant sense of self when I am coaching. I use the word *I* here, but I'm really just dedicated at the time to the dialogue with the client."

"When you are angry, who are you then?"

"Then I am angry. My experience of myself is that of being angry. I have judged that somebody has 'done me wrong' and I identify myself with that feeling of anger."

"Oh come on. Surely you can close your eyes and connect with some part of you that feels like Art. Isn't there some steadfast entity you call you?"

"Well, there is my self-image. I see myself as a likable fellow. I enjoy fine things. I am a nice guy. People call me generous. I am a father. I am this guy who does these things most of the time. Sure, I have a collective sense of me."

"But isn't there a self somewhere underneath all that? Some singularity, as you would put it?"

"Yes, I suppose. I can close my eyes and connect with a single sense of me."

"So self is real? It is not an illusion?"

"I honestly don't think there is something in the world that exists independently of my body that is my 'self.' I don't think it works that way. I think my brain produces an image of me. And for me, that image is real. But I can't pretend that image is real to you. Your image of you is real to you."

"Is this self part of the universe?"

"Do you mean in terms of space and time?"

"Yes."

"No. I don't personally believe it is an entity in the universe. I think it is a projection created by my brain."

"What about in some dimension that is bigger than space and time, but that contained space and time. Couldn't your self exist at that level?"

"I suppose so. But I tend to think not."

"So, if you wanted to become less of a worrier, in the same way that I want to, what would you do?"

"When I catch myself worrying, I would direct my attention to the fact that I was suffering from the illusion that I needed to worry. I would remind myself that it may indeed be prudent to consider what in the object world needs attention, but that I needn't go so wild over it. I would attempt to get a perspective on the matter. I would try to connect with the core feeling of fear that the situation was reminding me of. I would seek to feel that fear and try to embrace it as part of me."

"And then you would go through that process of locating the fear, maybe crying about it and settling with it. Right?"

"Right."

"So why have we talked about how meta-level thoughts have created the worry?"

"Good question. We did it so you would take worry bouts for what they are. I have been attempting to show you how things get out of proportion. We lose perspective. In a worry episode, there are the facts and then there are the fabricated reactions to the facts. The worry itself seems bigger to the worrier than the facts themselves. I thought it would be good for you to see the big picture. It's good to put things into perspective. Would you agree?"

"Yes, but when I'm actually worried, I know those things. I know that I have blown things out of perspective. Dealing with the feelings in the way that we have been talking about in these sessions is the only thing that seems to work."

"Good. And as time goes on, you will become more and more aware of the link between the things provoking the feelings and the fear you uncovered for yourself. Eventually you will be in front of a situation and actually catch yourself before you start to worry. And you will be able to make a choice. You'll stumble a few times. But eventually you will be able to choose not to run with the worry. You'll choose to go with your faith in yourself. Our discussion of the illusion of self is meant to speed up that process of learning to choose. By realizing the difference between facts and what we do with those facts, and by becoming more aware of the lack of foundation behind even our experience of self, you will probably get there a little faster."

"But it does present a frightening notion. Not only does my worry give me angst, the possibility of being much less than I thought I was is, well, bizarre."

"Ah. I can understand that. But don't worry. There is good news to come."

In Summary

Before we move on, let's collect some key points from this chapter:

- There are the facts of the world (e.g., you are reading this sentence), and there are the opinions of these facts (e.g., you accept or reject the point of the sentence).

- The reactions you have to the world that you would like to get better control of all come from your opinions or judgments.

- So, managing your judgments of the world will help you to manage your troublesome reactions.

- If you could just stay focused on the facts—the object-level—you'd be okay. But it's hard to do. It means getting control of your tendency to judge.

- Your ego judges for a living, always watching to see whether it likes what it's seeing.

- Your ego needs to "lighten up"—you take yourself too seriously!

- You operate as though all your opinions actually come from the world of facts. The realization that they don't come from the world of facts may help you gain mastery over your troublesome reactions.

CHAPTER 9

Our Shaky Foundations

Considering the picture being painted in this book, you may well be feeling a little insecure. After all, we have suggested that not only do your insecurities stem from intangible meta-level judgments, but so do you. We have said that your sense of self is a fabrication. Here you are trying to get a grip on the insecurities that make you one of the six types discussed in this book, and now you're being told that your sense of who you are rests on shaky foundations.

But fear not. After we finish exposing the sense of self for what it is, we will, in Part III of this book, rebuild. You will learn much more about how the shakiness of consciousness can empower you and help you find peace. We just have a little way to go before getting there.

Let's revisit the six types in the context of insecurity and fear:

1. Judith is a textbook *worrier.* When things happen on the job or at home that seem to come at her out of the blue, she goes into worry mode. She gets very anxious, to the point where she becomes a bit of a nuisance to those around her. When she worries, her angst looks her square in the eye and makes her squirm. Judith does not have to look far to see the shakiness of her foundations. She can see it in her own face.

2. Robbie is a *controlling* personality. He needs to get his way. He manipulates. He pushes. He forcefully steers people to do what he wants. If they go off course, he becomes all the more intense. For Robbie, being out of control would mean facing his deepest fear. His operating principle is that if he doesn't keep things together, they—he—will fall apart into some abyss.

3. Catherine is full of a sense of self-importance. People call her a *fake*, though, because to them she clearly does not qualify for the image she is so busy projecting. She behaves as if she is part of the intellectual elite and is one of those high-potential managers in the eyes of her company's executive team. But those around her see her as simply very political—all sizzle, no steak. Catherine does not seem to be in touch with who she really is. Behind her façade is a woman who is frightened. She feels insecure. She works very, very hard at moving away from that feeling. She is not in touch with that insecurity, but it drives her most of the time. Although it has made her what she is today, it also holds her back from finding peace within herself.

4. **Ruth is an** *attention-seeker.* She is always busy waving a personal flag so that people take notice of her in the crowd. She wants them to see that she is somehow different from the rest. Her effort to get their attention is a very deep, sincere craving to fill a gap. Her greatest fear is that she is not worth being seen at all. It makes her feel very insecure. She relies on other people to make her feel okay.

5. **Bob, a** *victim*, **is busy defending himself from culpability.** When he is involved in something that goes wrong, he quickly mounts a campaign—large or small—to establish his innocence. At the core he is fearful of taking blame because, to him, owning failure smells a lot like admitting to being nothing.

6. **Wayne is a** *prisoner* **of his anxieties.** He feels terrible when people are angry at him. He equates being the object of wrath with being absolutely unlovable. His fear is that he is not worthy of the love he so dearly craves. People can trigger his insecurity just by mentioning the word *angry*.

Meaning

These people all have something in common: a feeling of vulnerability. They crave a feeling of security. Each of them has overlaid a meaning onto the core tension between their feeling of vulnerability and their craving. They either aspire to fulfill this meaning, or they are plagued by their meaning and work to reject it.

Here are the three people from the above list who are *moving toward* the meaning they have produced:

- Catherine, the fake, finds meaning in the image she projects. She is trying to become this image.

- Ruth, the attention-seeker, finds her meaning is in what people see when she gets their attention.

- Robbie, the controller, pursues control in order to give meaning to his life.

The other three people are *moving away* from meaning they have produced:

- Judith, the worrier, finds meaning in the thing she worries about. Her brain is busy chewing on how to avoid the meaning she has created.

- Bob's meaning, as a victim, is what he is trying to avoid—responsibility for failure.

- Wayne's periodic prisoner status is what he hates. He shields his eyes from his personally produced painful meaning—that he is unlovable.

Picture yourself standing on a cliff overlooking the most sublime seaside panorama you can imagine. In the horizon the deep blue sky blends perfectly with the blue hues of the sea. Birds are flying playfully at the shoreline. There is a soft seaside breeze that, as you inhale deeply, fills your lungs with joy.

But behind you, things are different. You turn away from the beauty and you are startled by complete darkness. It is completely silent. It feels like emptiness. It is frighteningly without substance. Nothingness is staring you right in the face. It infects you with gloom.

Almost everybody in the world stands in this place. Those who are looking out to the sea have hell just over their shoulder. They sense it is right behind them. But they continue to look to the sun, hoping to forget what they know to be true. Those who are looking into the emptiness hate what they see. They are told to turn around, and sometimes they do. But not for long. They always look back. They can't help it. It's right there.

The Ultimate Paradox

The types we have been exploring who promote a certain image or position are the ones with nothingness just over their shoulder. The ones who have been attempting to reject the troublesome meaning they find in their world are the ones staring at nothingness, knowing that behind them lies the possibility of joy. They turn to see the beauty but are tugged back just the same.

Here's the ultimate paradox: Neither group can overcome their problem unless they step out of their paradigm. They must transcend. But the route to transcendence is to embrace their paradigm. Many religions, religious leaders, and philosophers have been making similar claims. For example, some Christians say if you give yourself to Jesus, then salvation is yours. There is a resignation required to gain admission. Some Buddhists say that to move past the pain of sitting in prolonged meditation, one must just continue to sit. Instead of changing positions, the meditator must move into the pain. The pain of sitting is a metaphor for the suffering of life. The temptation is to relieve the suffering, and the solution is to embrace it.

One has to climb over walls of self-protection to find release. But it doesn't have to be a religion that provides the boost. It may not have to pertain to God. It might simply just be about owning your fears—recognizing that they drive your primary troublesome behaviors, recognizing that you have understandably been resisting those fears—and then finding the courage to accept that the fears are a part of your life.

"It hurts," said Bertrum. "I don't want to move into that space."

Bertrum had come to see me because he was a prisoner—he was periodically taken captive by anxiety. A senior account person for a large telecommunications company, he was responsible for the big sales of the organization; his average transaction value was $250 million.

We spent time considering the possibility of his accepting that anxiety was a part of life. He was very reluctant. So we made a pact. The next time he was struck by his anxiety, he would call me and we would work it through together. He warned me that I might find him at the other end of my phone at an odd hour of the day. That's fine, I told him.

The phone rang at 6:30 P.M. as I was sitting down for dinner with my family. It was Bertrum.

"This is it, I've got it right now," he said. "Are you free?"

"Sure," I said. My daughter held the phone while I went to the family room to take the call. She hung up when I came back on the line.

"What happened?" I asked.

"Well, I'm home right now. Before having dinner I called my voice mail to check for messages. I got one from a huge prospective client. He was complaining about how some of our engineers behaved when they were doing some research today. Apparently they were rude to some of his staff. He suggested that if that's how our team behaved, things might not work out."

"And then what happened?"

"Well, I felt that tightness in my chest and decided to call you."

"Good." I said. "Are you alone right now?"

"Yes."

"Okay. I want you to close your eyes and tell me what you feel."

"I feel that tightness."

"Put your hand there. And press down a bit, just to really get connected to your body."

"Okay, I'm pressing."

"Can you tell me what emotion you feel?"

"I'm scared," he said in a cynical kind of way, as if the hand thing was a bit much. "I really need this deal. We've been through such hell over the last while. You have no idea. I'm sick and tired of all the ups and downs. This will probably work out, but it's a vulnerability. Do you know what I mean?"

"Yes. Tell me more about how you feel."

The next thing he said went not to the potential of a lost sale but to his fear of the anxiety itself. He was reporting his resistance to move into his dark space.

"It hurts. I don't want to move into that space."

"Go there, Bertrum."

I could hear him kind of grunt at the other end of the phone. And then he said, "I'm so tired of the fight."

"What are you fighting against?"

"I'm so afraid."

Now he was really getting it out. I gave him some time.

"I'm afraid it's all going to fall apart. And then I'll be nothing. Absolutely nothing." After another pause, he said, "They won't love me. And it wasn't my fault. All that I've built will fall apart. It hurts so much, Art. This is it. The tightness is my fear of failure. My fear of losing my position. My fear of starting from scratch."

"Bertrum," I said, "I would like you to hold on to that fear for a short while. Right now. With me on the phone. I want you to know that you have this fear in you all the time. Usually it's tucked away somewhere, but it's in there. In fact, I would suggest you work so hard because of this fear. You spend all of your time protecting against it. And when it looks like it's coming out, you tighten up. I want you to know that this deep fear is the same fear that I have and that your wife has and that even that customer has. It is human fear. Own it. Don't push it away. Consider for a moment how it motivates you; how it drives much of what you do. Do you know what I mean?"

"Yes, I think so," he said in a calmer voice. "It is inside my sentences when I talk. It is in my head when I'm up late at night working on spreadsheets. It is in my voice when I'm presenting. It is my hard work. It's like everything I do is somehow the outbound flow after an explosion. You know how when a bomb goes off, things fly away from the center of the explosion?"

"Well, only sort of, but I think I know what you mean," I said.

Bertrum understood his anxiety. His fear was deep. It charged him up and flowed out through his day-to-day life. In one sense it motivated him. In another he was hiding from it. It was just behind him, always peering over his shoulder.

When he heard the message prior to calling me, the thing he was hiding from was actually coming straight toward him. It was terrifying.

"We're not done yet, Bertrum," I said. "We really do need you to incorporate your understanding into your awareness, so that you are less vulnerable in the future."

"How do we do that?"

"Well, we're seeing each other in a couple of days, right?"

"Yes."

"Between now and then, I want you to keep a little diary that you access every hour or so. Enter into the diary the things you were doing over the previous hour, and in point form indicate the way in which they are a manifestation of your fear. I want you to learn about how that fear is a driver and how it is very real and a part of your life. When we see each other next, we'll review the diary and talk about how to accept the fear."

"Okay."

I knew what would happen when I saw Bertrum next. It almost always happens with this exercise. He would show up with regular diary entries for the first several hours and then sporadic entries after that. The dying out of entries would not be because he got lazy or bored. It would be because the entries were becoming redundant. Bertrum would (and did) start the session with a statement or two about how it became very obvious to him that, in a sense, he was fear. And that it was somehow okay.

Bertrum's object-level thoughts on the night he called me had gathered information from the voice-mail message. His meta-level thoughts had rapidly drawn links between this information and possible outcomes, and he had projected a worst-case scenario. He judged the data to be very undesirable. He identified himself with his fear. His body experienced the fear response: muscle tightening and probably an elevation in pulse and blood pressure. His worst fears might come true.

To work through the core fear, he had to become comfortable with the notion that everything would be okay even if the worst case did happen. Rather than hiding from the fear, he had to confront it and relax with it. He had to spend time with it and make peace with it and himself. Accepting a fear can simply equate to allowing yourself to feel it for a while, slowly learning that the worst-case scenario, though undesirable, is livable, and acknowledging that fear is part of life. It involves a kind of resignation.

However, accepting fear does not mean to give in to it per se. Resignation does not have to mean losing. It only calls for realizing that a battle has been waged, that one has been immersed in the battle, that the battle is normal, and that the battle can be observed without the judgment of whether it is good or bad.

By learning to accept his worst fear, Bertrum relaxed. It was not an overnight transition, however. I'm sure he is still at it, infusing his awareness of the shakiness of his foundations into his day-to-day consciousness. But he got better and better during the course of our relationship.

Nothingness

Bertrum's reference to "nothingness" during our dinnertime telephone dialogue was no accident. I think he was pointing to a universal fear of what I have heard referred to as insubstantiality or emptiness. The idea is that there is nothing underneath the sense of self. Or, more precisely, the meta-level of consciousness has placed a singular image of the self, based on an array of inputs, on top of nothing.

The phenomenon can be likened to how a video projector projects a film at a movie theater. The object-level represents inputs to the projector: the film entering the machine. It contains all of the information available to render the picture. The meta-level is the series of lenses, mirrors, and lights that send the image into the theater. It takes the object-level data and creates a "thing" out of it. It's not a real thing, it's just an image being projected on a screen. That image is the self. It is being projected onto the screen. It looks real. It tempts us, as any good movie does, to get lost in its projected reality.

But if the lightbulb inside the projector blows, then the whole thing stops. There is nothing on the screen. It's blank. The audience's illusion of participating in the life being told on the screen is completely shattered. The machine is still running, but there is no "self."

I would suggest that people have an active projector running in their heads. They are in the audience, getting lost in the show. They are only vaguely aware that they are participating in an illusion. In fact, some people actually judge the show by how much of a distraction it created in their lives. They like to get lost in the program. A blank screen is not what they came for. They want the full image. The bigger the screen, the better. The big, bright picture is what it's all about. Darkness is bad.

We are very much afraid of a dark, blank screen. But without the projector doing its job, that's what's there. We fill that screen, with the best action, comedy, and drama programs that we can find. We fill the screen with meaning.

Sometimes when I go to an early matinee at a cinema complex with many screens I find an unoccupied, dark theater and go sit inside so that

I can see the blank screen and embrace the nothingness for a few moments. I find it invigorating to give physicality to the metaphor. Shutting off the meta-level meaning maker for a little while can indeed be refreshing. The object-level can be very satisfying in itself. Meta-level meaning can be such a heavy thing.

The meta-level compensates to some extent for the insubstantiality of consciousness by producing meaning. We can get hope from meaning. It picks us up when we are down. At any given moment, we have the security of whatever is on our mind (unless it's a negative thing on our mind). When we extend our thoughts into the future, insecurity can hit. That's when we need something to prop us up.

Some people use religion for that purpose. They have faith in God, and they use the various tenets of their religion to deal with things that would otherwise scare the pants off them. For example, people respond to expressions of fear that start with the words, "But what about . . ." with the words, "We'll have to trust God to handle that." I sometimes think that what that really communicates is the response, "I don't have the faintest idea, but if we allow ourselves to run with the possibility you are asking about, we haven't got a hope."

Self-esteem is a kind of meaning we experience. It means that we fully believe ourselves able and worthy. With high self-esteem, we have hope. With low self-esteem, we lack hope. We seek it from other sources.

Other meta-level creations get us through periods of hopelessness. The love we have for a partner, or for humanity, can be a source of inspiration to get us through tough times. In this case, we are leaning on those feelings to fuel our motivation.

In business, we have mission and vision statements to keep our spirit from falling through the cracks. In our personal lives, we have our dreams and our routines.

Goals give us a sense of hope. They give us a feeling that there is somewhere to aim for. And they work! They inspire. They provide a sense that things are under control. With goals and just a little progress toward them, there is no need to despair.

Some people seem like hope-producing machines. I know a man who is involved in multiple business ventures. All of them get him pumped up because they have not yet matured, so there is still hope that they will. Multiple, unfinished ventures are like lottery tickets whose winning numbers have not yet been chosen. One still feels the excitement of the possibility of winning.

But sometimes, we lose hope. Unless there is something to prop us up, there may well be a natural tendency for the meta-level dream machine to break down. In the view of Dr. Mihaly Csikszentmihalyi, professor and former chairman of the psychology department at the University of Chicago, consciousness, over time, tends to break down toward a state of disorder. The suggestion is that without certain conditions being met, hope, mood, and orderliness of thought will disintegrate.

It could be argued that one of the purposes of leadership is to compensate for the natural human tendency of people to get negative. Leaders offer us optimism, direction, mission, vision, and inspiration. Without their propping us up, our attitudes could spiral down to negativity and disorder.

Of course, there is nothing inherently wrong with keeping on track by relying on our leaders, our spirituality, our goals, and our self-produced belief that we are able and worthy. It's the way we operate. But now, when the reliance on these sources is not enough, or when there is a desire to get to the bottom of problems with the behaviors that define the six types explained in this book, we can add to the list the powerful idea discussed in this chapter: embracing our insubstantiality.

CHAPTER 10

How We Judge

Like forest rangers on the lookout for fires, we continually monitor our-selves for whether we have a problem. Our meta-level thought is always assessing how things are going at the object-level and motivating us to make changes based on its judgments. The judgments we make are meant to protect us.

- In the case of *worriers*, their meta-level judgments are detecting from the array of facts in front of them that it's time to become tightly focused on anticipating and avoiding what might happen.

- The meta-level judgments of *controllers* deem things to be out of control and indicate it's time to take charge.

- *Fakes* are motivated by their meta-level thoughts to project a cer-tain image—to cover up their real self-image.

- The meta-level awareness of *attention-seekers* tells them that things don't quite feel secure and looks for the right opportunity to fill the gap.

- The meta-level thoughts of *victims* stand on guard to protect them from attacks.

- *Prisoners* take meta-level indications of vague, hard-to-pin-down threats as a signal to check back into the "safety" of their prisons.

Meta-Level Judgments

We make judgments to try to help ourselves, but sometimes they cause us trouble. Our meta-level judging faculty can be trigger-happy. This is the source of the problem for many people who regret their emotional responses. In certain circumstances they know intellectually that their feelings are not appropriate—that they represent an overreaction of some sort—but they find it difficult not to pull the trigger.

But how do we judge? Let's answer this question with a real-life example: you. As you read these pages, your brain is taking in information. At the same time that you are absorbing the meaning at the object-level, you are busy at the meta-level assessing whether you like it, or agree with it. You are making judgments. I am doing the same thing as I am writing it. "This sounds too simple," either you or I might think. I personally just reread something and thought, "That was a poorly written paragraph." My wife recently read a part of the manuscript and while reading spoke her judgment out loud: "This is unclear."

All three statements above are judgments. They were made at the meta-level of consciousness. They may look like factual, object-level judgments, but they are meta-level judgments. For example, when someone says, "This sounds too simple," the word *too* reveals that, in this case, simplicity is undesirable. Or, when my wife says something is unclear, there is an implicit statement: "And that's not okay."

Judgments can actually be broken into two categories: factual judgments and value judgments:

1. *Factual judgments* **are about the object-level world.** They can be disputed, of course. But they can also be proved or disproved. Factual judgments are usually reliable. And if people can resist the temptation to depart from the world of facts into the world of generalizations and value judgments, there would be far fewer sources of tension in the world. "Nothing but the facts, ma'am," is the police officer's plea for holding back judgment while all relevant information is collected.

2. *Value judgments,* **however, contain an extra component.** They are meta-level creations that import things like goodness and badness, and desirability and undesirability. When we make value judgments, we are no longer pointing to facts; we have created a new entity to join the facts: our opinion about them.

Sometimes people hide value judgments inside factual statements. For example, "Bob has been late for four morning meetings in a row" sounds like a statement of fact. But the people hearing the comment made by Bob's boss know that inside the observation is a judgment that equates to "and that, my friends, as we all know, is simply not okay." And of course we're all aware of statements made about people (their ethnicity, body type, marital status, etc.) that seem factual on the surface but actually hide prejudicial value judgments.

The value judgments we make about people and situations are often the cause of our problems. If we could stop ourselves before making them, we would have a better chance of avoiding the behaviors that define the six types described in this book. We would also avoid hurting the feelings of others.

Communication "Sins"

There are several "sins" in communication that belong to the family of value judgments. They are all one or more steps away from the facts. For example, it's a fact that my colleague submitted a report to a client containing six spelling mistakes. Let's look at ways that I could embellish that fact with an unharnessed meta-level consciousness. To do so, we'll consider three dimensions: the concept itself, the person, and time.

1. *Conceptual exaggeration* would involve my saying, "My colleague makes a lot of mistakes," or "She communicates poorly." In both cases, something presumably related to spelling skills has been extended beyond the facts at hand. I could even go so far as to say, "My colleague is unprofessional." The key is that I have applied a pejorative generalization pertaining to the topic of making spelling mistakes.

2. *Personalization* of value judgments is the most hurtful of all. In this example, I would say specifically of the colleague, "This colleague is a bad speller," or "This colleague is unprofessional." These sorts of generalizations are the most hurtful because they are begging for some kind of identification of the person with the sin. The use of the verb *to be* is what causes the problem. To say somebody is anything in particular is not only incomplete, it might irrationally pigeonhole that person and cause damage to her reputation.

3. *Temporal exaggeration* is about time. If I said, "She always makes

spelling mistakes," then I would have suggested that this is a recurring phenomenon. I might make this an observation about the past, a prediction of the future, or both.

All of the above judgments qualify as value judgments because they allude to some undesirable aspect of what is being judged. They would also have been value judgments if they had alluded only to favorable aspects of the person and behavior. Negative value judgments not only hurt people but they also can get the person who is casting the judgment into trouble. Most managers know that when you criticize someone it is important not to label or generalize.

It is not necessarily irrational, or inappropriate, to make such statements, however. Sometimes we need to point out patterns to people so they get the point. The key is to remain focused on what is necessarily or very likely true. It is probably not true that my colleague is unprofessional simply because of several spelling mistakes on submitted documents. It may be appropriate to say that there is an "emerging spelling issue" that needs attention. After all, the job of a leader includes the development of the people being led.

What we are interested in under the heading of managing our tendency to worry, control, fake, seek attention, deflect blame, or imprison ourselves is how we make judgments that push our own buttons. These kinds of value judgments also extend over space, time, and the individual, regardless of whether we utter them or not. For example, if I become worried every time a prospective client chooses another supplier instead of my own firm, it is probably because I am extending the single rejection into the future. I may be taking the one rejection and extending it temporally by saying, "We'll never get a new client." Or, I may extend such rejection conceptually and say, "Whenever we try to get new business we fail." Finally, under the context of personalization, I may say to myself, "The truth is, we are no good; we are failures."

Some people blow things way out of proportion by combining their exaggerations. For example, regarding the consecutive spelling mistakes, I might say, "This woman is an idiot who can't spell and can't communicate professionally—she never could and she never will." In this statement I have moved from spelling mistakes to aspersions about the woman's intelligence, competence, and professional future.

As a matter of fact, there are various factors that determine how much a person will generalize: how emotional he feels at the time, his stress levels, his personal habits, and the habits of the people around him doing the generalizing. It is easy to generalize. It is difficult to stay with specifics.

The Unspoken Gap Analysis

When we judge, an unspoken gap analysis is going on. For example, we compare the present with some desired state. The gap between these two depicts how much work we have to do to make things right. The interesting thing is where the defined desired state comes from.

Throughout our lives we are building some image in our mind of the way we think things ought to be. Our parents set these standards. So do our teachers, our friends, our religions, our employers, and the media. Think of a young person coming home from school after learning from his peers what "cool" means. In the morning, he had left home with no idea that cool people wear certain running shoes. By evening, he is making the pronouncement that anybody who doesn't wear those shoes is simply not cool.

All of us have an image of how the world ought to be. And we are constantly comparing that image with what's in front of us. And we judge accordingly. Many of our gap analyses are in reverse. We want a gap. We know where we don't want to be and we determine that this is pretty much where we are, so we judge the situation undesirable.

There is an upside to generalizations. They do help us. Personally, I don't lean on stove tops. It's just a thing of mine. When I was a kid, I leaned on a stove top and was burned. From that point on, well, I've been prejudiced about all stove tops. If there's a stove top, I don't lean. Simple. My rule about stove tops saves me time, trouble, and the possibility of being burned by one. The key to generalizing is that we have to be careful so that we avoid hurting somebody's feelings or forfeiting an unknown opportunity for fear of the risk involved.

The Risks of Judging

Twenty years ago I was facilitating a management seminar for a small group of junior and midlevel leaders in a large, brand-name company. The session was partly dedicated to helping the group develop their hiring skills. I lost that client abruptly after my session on how to choose which candidates to interview for a job opening.

How did that happen? I remember saying to the group that when you run an ad for employees you will build a pile of résumés that will need to be sifted through in order to short-list candidates worth an interview.

"There is a role for a certain amount of rational discrimination here," I said. "It's useful to go through the résumés and weed out people who simply don't understand the importance of putting forth a good image. So, go through the stack and when you see a document that was poorly photocopied (in those days, only hard copies were submitted by candidates) or that has spelling mistakes, move it to the 'no way' pile."

The HR person who had procured my services got in touch with me after the session and said, "I'm sorry, but I don't think our values are aligned. We are totally against discrimination in this organization."

"But discrimination is how people learn," I replied. "We see patterns and we become prejudiced!"

Her response was that she couldn't afford to engage the services of someone who espoused any kind of discrimination.

Ironically, this person was employing a prejudice against me. She moved from what I said about screening résumés and extended it to a bunch of other areas. In her head was the belief that people who say certain things are more likely to say certain other things. I'm against all stove tops and she's against people who overtly encourage certain types of discrimination.

Certain triggers, when pressed, dictate conclusions that, though not guaranteed, save time and trouble. For example, when someone in authority says something, we are more likely to conclude that it may well be true. When we perceive that something that is not widely available is becoming in short supply, we extend the pattern to judge that we have a problem if we don't act quickly. When people do us favors, we extend the pattern to think that they can be trusted. When people have a few things in common with us, we extend the pattern to the possibility of friendship. These triggers speed up our judgments and, though they do present a risk of being wrong, simplify our lives.

Whether we compare the present with an ideal or with what unfortunate thing might happen, we have laid the basis for value judgments. The main point is that our value judgments may not be rational. They employ inductive logic in that they move from pieces of individual evidence to generalizations about all such cases. But we don't have all the possibilities accounted for. The risk of this kind of reasoning is the possibility of misapplying the generalization to a new case.

My son can eat a hot dog with ketchup and mustard smeared all the way up his arm without giving a hoot. There is no ideal in his mind about goo smeared on skin, so for him, goo is not a problem. Further, there is no belief that goo is a bad thing, so seeing new goo is not a bad thing. My son is free of value judgment when it comes to the intricacies of hot dog consumption. If you called my son a "slob" over the matter, it would be extending the smear onto his humanity, and it could hurt (though in his case, I doubt it). People generally don't like being labeled.

A woman on my team asked me for some feedback on her performance. I said I thought she was intellectually lazy. She was deeply hurt. Her morale dropped. She felt she had been pigeonholed. It's true that her own vulnerability led to her problem; after all, she didn't have to run with the label and assume it was hers forever. But I learned a lesson. My statement was a little stupid. Even if I believed it was true of her, I should have known that there was a big risk in saying it. In fact, I could have communicated the issue with much more finesse. For example, I could have said, "Marissa, I'd like you to spend more time doing personal research so that we can hear some of your own thoughts on some of these subjects. You'll get such a pleasure if you read juicy material that sheds a light on some of these topics! And if you share it with us, we'll all be better off."

So our meta-level thoughts are very busy passing judgments in order to save us time and trouble and to help us survive and thrive. We ought to be grateful. But they also engage us in our problems. The six types discussed in this book are plagued by the effects of their judgments. So they need to make their judgments in context. The realization that judgments can be premature will make them a little less susceptible to their allure.

Where Ego Steps In

Meta-level judgments usually come from ego, the part of us that wants us to find more security and to avoid insecurity. These are often the criteria for our judgments. When our ego is not engaged, we tend to stay at the object-level, dealing with facts as they emerge.

When we label someone as having done us harm, our ego is engaged. Accordingly, forgiveness is difficult to access. It involves relaxing the ego response presumably triggered by their behavior and going back to an object-level observation.

I introduced my friend Saul to a client of mine so that Saul could earn some money to tide him over during a period of unemployment. Saul learned my client's business in a couple of months and then quit this temporary job to start up a new company in direct competition with my client.

When I heard this it was as if someone had dropped a bag of bricks on me. I quickly judged Saul to be unethical. My meta-level thoughts pegged him as devious. I had a real problem entertaining the notion of forgiving Saul. As far as I was concerned, I had introduced Saul to my client to help Saul. His decision to take advantage of my gesture and do something that was harmful to my client was "unforgivable."

I was stuck in my judgment. Over time, I got past my judgment. My client tried to make me understand that, in his view, nature was simply taking its course. My wife helped me realize that my friendship with Saul was important to me. I came to see that the situation did not merit the judgment I was applying. My original meta-view was that friends don't hurt the friends of their friends. But if I had stayed at the object-level I would have seen that Saul was legally free to do what he did. He needed money and felt he had come across a viable opportunity. He went for it. He started a business after learning about an industry in which he thought he could thrive. My client was not tangibly hurt, and he was not angry at me. So was it so bad? I made up with my friend.

When someone has erred, we often apply *internal attribution* to that person. For example, I initially claimed that it was Saul who committed the offense. It was his devious personality that caused it. However, when we ourselves err, we are more likely to apply *external attribution*, attributing causes to situational factors rather than blaming ourselves. It was not likely that I would take any blame for the Saul fiasco. But maybe, in fact, I was to blame. After all, I didn't lay out any ground rules for him. I didn't advise my client to protect himself.

So our judgment comes early in the sequence of events that lead to or away from our anxieties. Something happens, and we leap to our inductive conclusions. For example, when there are signs of layoffs in our industry, we extend these object-level notions to the possibility of layoffs affecting us personally. Our buttons get pressed.

There are two main types of negative responses: judgments that lead us to the perceived angst and judgments that attempt to move us away from it. Half of our six problematic types discussed in this book are victims of an angst they consciously perceive. The other three types are caught up in angst avoidance. *Perceiving angst* leads to worry and victim thinking and the response of the prisoner. *Avoiding angst* is what the controller, the fake, and the attention-seeker do.

Perceiving Angst

■ *Worriers* are people who experience angst as the result of their judgments. Worriers fret. They believe there is something ahead of them that will bring doom down on their heads. Their meta-thought has created a picture of a possible bad outcome, and they can't seem to take their eyes off it. When they identify themselves with the fear, they lose sight of the objects themselves. There may indeed be something out there to be afraid of, but getting lost in the fear is like believing in ghosts. But there are no ghosts in the world. There are only objects.

■ *Prisoners* also perceive anxiety, only in their case they sometimes don't really know what their eyes are stuck on. They just know that they have made a judgment based on some conflict between how they want things to be and how they actually are. Getting engrossed in the feeling that flowed from the judgment means losing sight of the facts and dwelling on the intangible.

■ *Victims* are people whose meta-level consciousness has judged that there is a possibility of blame being levied on them. They move to resist the judgment. But there is no blame in the world. Blame is not an object. It is no more tangible than a self. Both are constructs of the meta-world.

Avoiding Angst

Those who avoid their angst by looking away—controllers, attention-seekers, and fakes—are also subscribing to the existence of ghosts. All constructs of meta-thoughts are useful entities because they give us tools to survive. But when we become driven by them, lost in them, we let them take us too far.

■ *Controllers* make their judgments and then derive fuel from them to get control. They get lost in their effort to get their own way, motivated by a self-produced angst.

■ *Attention-seekers'* meta-level thoughts create out of the blue a sense of emptiness, judge that this emptiness is just not okay, and look away while they try to fill it with other people's sense of who they are.

■ *Fakes*, people who feel a dissonance between what they know about themselves and how they behave, judge themselves very unfavorably while they continue to sustain the falsehood.

We're All Fakes

To some extent, given that we all operate on the assumption that self exists as a separate entity, even though we know that since it is a meta-level construct, it does not really exist, we must all operate as fakes. We must operate in the world even though we really cannot pin down just who is doing the operating.

Let's look at an example of the judgments that we fakes make.

Lucinda wakes up every morning about two hours before she has to leave so that she can do all the sprucing up she thinks is necessary to look right for her job. Lucinda judges herself, usually unconsciously—though sometimes painfully consciously—as unattractive. Of course, at the object-level, there is no such thing as unattractive. It is a subjective judgment that Lucinda makes, regardless of how society defines attractive. So, that's her ghost. She ascribes "ugliness" to herself even though there is no real ugliness in the object world.

Then she goes about her day meeting people and being sociable, while privately and unconsciously holding on to the belief that she does not deserve their attention because she is ugly. She feels torn between what she believes about herself and how she behaves. She doesn't accept herself for what she is. She doesn't accept her looks.

When Lucinda receives a compliment, her first reaction is to deflect it. She does so both publicly and privately. Her public response to a compliment is to say something like, "Oh, you're very kind. But no—it's really nothing special." Her private response is to reject the compliment outright and then to judge the other person as being a fraud. No compliment could ever speak the truth about Lucinda, as far as she is concerned.

So she goes about her days leading a kind of double life. She behaves as though she looks normal while privately thinking she is ugly. And she feels great angst over the hypocrisy.

Consider how Lucinda is lost in a world of constructs:

- First, she is not ugly. She just is. Her value judgment against her appearance has gone too far.

- Second, she compares herself with what she thinks others define as good looking, but that "good lookingness" doesn't really exist either. It's just an artificial construct.

- Third, she judges herself to be a hypocrite because of the alleged falsity and feels significant angst about it. She judges herself over constructs, in some kind of meta-meta manner. Lucinda's judgments have taken her out of the world of objects.

We cannot and should not dispense with the meta-level judgments we make. But it would be smart to balance them, to keep them in perspective. Actually, in my coaching and managerial work, I am most impressed by people who acknowledge the fakery of their lives and continue in the inevitable fakery of life. Their acknowledgment of their fakery is the key. When we don't acknowledge our fakery, we participate in a bad faith, in a lie we tell to ourselves. We lie to ourselves when we assume our value judgments are necessarily true. We say, "It's my opinion, so it is allowed." Well, it is allowed, but don't lose sight of what it is.

Many of us would benefit greatly from shining a light on the lies we tell to ourselves. Doing so would help us break free of the illusions we hang on to.

Think of a man who does the same job for fifteen years and never advances to the next level. He tells himself he's good at what he does. He provides well for his family. He's never surprised by what faces him on Monday mornings, because he's seen it all. These are good things.

What he avoids, however, is the truth that lies deep inside him, the truth that he's grown completely apathetic and halfhearted about his job. It doesn't fill him up anymore. It doesn't challenge him. Yet he's convinced himself that it's okay because of all the positives it provides. By doing so, he denies himself other possibilities that exist, possibilities that he will never see if he continues in his status quo. Were he to acknowledge the truth of his situation, admitting that he is bored and dissatisfied, he would cause an agency to well up within him, a sense of urgency to move. It would allow him to be true to himself, would cause him to take the necessary action to change his life.

For me, the truth is that there are objects in the world and there are my opinions about those objects. My opinions come across to me as though they are the truth. So, too, does my sense of self give me the feeling of being substantial. I need my opinions to operate. I need my sense of self to operate. But my growth depends on getting some perspective on these things. Humility is good. It sets the stage for progress in overcoming the behaviors possessed by the types defined in this book. They too derive from the meta-world of opinion, meaning, and self.

PART III

Moving from Fear to Freedom

CHAPTER 11

What's Your Operating Strategy?

We have examined in detail the six types in whose ranks we or those with whom we work may number. And we have explored ourselves using the Transcendence Model. We are now better able to understand our present status and future possibilities. Continuing this trend, it's time to define our individual operating strategies. Doing so will help us move from the fear that causes conflict within and without to a wonderful freedom in our work and in our lives.

As a prelude to defining our operating strategies, let us review how we are programmed to act.

A program in your brain—we called it meta-level thinking—creates and projects your sense of self onto your consciousness. It's like a movie projector projecting its picture onto a blank screen. This same program creates meaning in your life. It is also very busy assessing everything that's going on and judging whether it likes what it sees.

This assessment activity is critical for your survival. It allows you to make rapid decisions as your fast-paced, stressful days go whizzing by. If it says, "I don't trust that man," then you act accordingly. It takes the facts as you see them and makes value judgments. The output, the stuff projected onto the screen—self, meaning, and judgments—are not part of the object world. They don't depict what is tangible. They point to artificially constructed ghosts. The ghosts are critical for our survival, insofar as the judgments they make help us operate in the world—but they are ghosts nonetheless.

Your feelings of security are the meta-level's primary motivator. To make its judgments, it assesses whether something will help you feel

159

secure or will make you feel insecure. For example, if you are in a meeting with your boss and she wants to change the method you've chosen for attacking a certain project and you really want to do it your way, then your thoughts will go to, "I don't like this." They may even go to some generalization like, "my boss always does that," or "she is a control freak," or "she doesn't let me do anything my way."

Your meta-level judgments have a pattern to them. The pattern concerns what you are usually watching for when you see or hear new things.

- The *worrier* is usually watching for the thing she fears the most.

- The *controller* is usually watching for whether things are going her way.

- The *fake* is usually watching for whether his illusion is being sustained.

- The *attention-seeker* is watching for opportunities to strut his stuff.

- The *victim* is watching for whether blame is on its way.

- The *prisoner* is watching for some sign that a past trauma might return or that some beliefs may prove true.

The visual phrase "watching for" is not the only possible descriptor. You might say, "listening for" or "taste testing" or "scanning for" or "checking to see if." The idea is that the meta-level is always on guard duty. It checks, judges, and motivates you into specific actions.

Detecting Your Operating Strategy

This process of checking, judging, and acting in order to achieve a personal ambition is your operating strategy. You employ such a strategy most of the time. It is not all that your meta-level is up to, but it is one of its most active programs.

By the end of this chapter you will have used some self-reflection to define your operating strategy. You will end up with a few sentences that summarize what you check for, the kind of judgments you reach, and how and why you tend to act on those judgments. You may be struck by how simple it is. You may also be struck by how profound it is.

Keep these four questions in mind as you read along, and at some point take a few minutes to address them:

1. What do you tend to be checking on as you observe and listen to things?
2. How do you make this determination? What kind of factors do you consider?
3. When your checking uncovers what you are seeking, in what types of action do you engage?
4. Why do you act in this way?

My own operating strategy works like this: I am continually checking for whether I sense a block in other people's thinking. I do this by listening for gaps in their stories. If I determine that there is such a block or gap, I help them remove it. Doing this makes me feel powerful and lovable. On the one hand, the simplicity of this startles me. I know it is accurate, but it feels very strange to both discover it and expose it. On the other hand, the extent to which it explains a lot of what I do is amazing. My family's chorus in response to this disclosure would definitely be, "Yes! That's you to a tee. You are always looking for how people are screwed up and then presuming to help. It drives us crazy."

It's a little embarrassing for me to expose my operating strategy. It implies that all I do is look for blocks in people and attempt to remove them. What a machine! It makes me seem so simple and perhaps even narcissistic. After all, what makes me engage in such a strategy may be a sincere desire to help people, but it clearly is also the means for my feeling fulfilled. I like to help other people because it makes me feel good. I seem to think it will make them think I'm powerful and maybe cause them to love me back.

Knowing your operating strategy will explain many of the things you do. Mine explains why I do what I do for a living. Does yours?

You can thank your operating strategy for what you have attained so far in your career. After all, you are in your current position because your style of operating on the job revealed your capabilities to your manager or senior management. The upside of being a worrier, for example, is that you take things seriously enough to be motivated to find solutions.

Controllers do gain control, and if they are effective, their control wins them successes. Attention-seekers do indeed get attention and often this is all it takes to make it in the world. Victims have learned to watch out for blame because, at least a few times, it freed them from culpability. The list goes on.

But your operating strategy is also what is holding you back from being more than what you are today. That's the problem with an operating strategy. Once you have it defined, you'll realize that while it may well explain your current behavior, it may also be limiting you because it means you are not checking for other things. For example, let's say you are a victim. Your operating strategy demands that you check to see whether things are under control. If they are not under control, you work to demonstrate how it is not your fault so you are free of blame. By definition, then, you are not checking for other things. For instance, you might miss that other people are in need and how you can help. You are otherwise occupied.

If your strategy is holding you back, you might derive some value from adding to it and tweaking it. You could say, in the case of the previous example, "I check whether things are under control and whether others are happy. If things are not under control or if people are not happy, then I act to soothe people and locate a cause so the problem won't recur." In this case, the modification to your operating strategy will help you check for two things and redirect your reaction. Consequently, you will focus less on how you are not to blame and more on what can be done about the problems you detect.

Your ego is the natural source of your operating strategy. Your ego works to move you to greater security. It is very motivated. For example, if you are an attention-seeker, you may be constantly checking for whether you are loved. If you judge that you are not loved, you may be moved to influence others one way or another in order to impress them. This is one way to describe what the ego does for a living. It finds a way to move you toward greater security and away from insecurity.

Once you have your operating strategy labeled, you may well choose to continue with it. Nobody is demanding otherwise. The idea is that by knowing that it is yours, you empower yourself to change it if you wish and you overcome some degree of personal bad faith. That is, you don't have to play a game where you pretend your motives are otherwise. You know your operating strategy and you give yourself permission to employ it. A client of mine concluded, for example, that his operating strategy was to check for opportunities to be a hero. If he judged that there was such an opportunity, he would get into gear to be a hero and then be loved. He learned that this was his modus operandi, and he concluded that though it was his automatic programming, it wasn't so bad. He knew what game he was playing. He knew it worked for him.

To some extent, playing out an operating strategy may be a bit of a game. It could imply narcissism or a lack of authenticity. For example, you and others may think you are compassionately listening to someone, but you may just be satisfying some programmed need to listen so that you can perform some function other than simply lending a hand when someone is in need. Perhaps you are busy looking for opportunities to sound intelligent. You may project compassion, but your ulterior motive may be somewhat more selfish. You want the attention.

On the other hand, having an operating strategy does not necessarily mean you are lost in some pernicious program. For instance, I know many parents who are always checking to see whether their kids are in need, and, if they judge that to be the case, they quickly move to make things right so they feel they've been acting responsibly.

Some people have an operating strategy at work that is different from home. This is fairly common among mothers. At work they may be checking for vulnerability to various possible political attacks, while at home they are engaged in nothing but expressions of love in order to keep the family happy and healthy.

Some people have a conditional operating strategy. They first check for one thing, and then, if there is no issue requiring attention, they check for some other, secondary thing. I know a man who first looks for whether the people he cares about are okay. If they are not okay, he moves to make things better. If they are fine, he checks for what task is incomplete. If he can lend a hand to finish a task, he proceeds to do so.

Conditional operating strategies are often used by people who have adopted some kind of temporary but important mission. For example, when profits are down and there is a directive about cost savings, then fiscal feasibility is often the first condition that must be satisfied for someone listening to other people talking about their plans. If the plans are fiscally feasible, they move to whatever is their default position.

Defining Your Operating Strategy

The following three questions will help you define your operating strategy:

1. What are you checking on? You can source what you tend to be checking on by working backward from the problematic behaviors that have motivated you to read this far in this book. For example, let's say you tend to get hooked every time you must confront someone. That might tell you that you are frequently checking for whether you are safe or whether you are loved. Or, if you tend toward controlling behavior, perhaps you frequently check whether people are doing things in the way that you define as right. Victims might be checking for what went wrong so that they can preempt any blame before it strikes.

2. What triggers your judgment? Once you get a grip on what you are checking on during your day, direct your attention to what kinds of things trigger the judgment that you are in a problem situation. It is one thing to know that you listen for whether you are loved, but it is another thing altogether to know what exactly triggers your anxiety. Perhaps you come to the conclusion that you are not loved by others when you hear someone start to say "no" to your requests. Or, maybe you reach this conclusion when people argue with you. Or when people make jokes in your presence. Or when they don't readily go along with your ideas. Knowing exactly what triggers your judgment makes you more aware when you are tempted to reach the same judgment in the future.

3. What's your behavioral trend? The final step in sorting out your operating strategy concerns defining your behavioral trend What do you tend to do once you have been triggered into action by your judgment? Do you take control? Do you move to defend? Do you ridicule others? Do you clean up? Cook? Eat? Hide? Fight? Get lazy?

Here is a dialogue I had with a person who wanted to understand her operating strategy. Judy is an operations director in a credit card–

processing organization. She leads a team of seven managers, who in turn lead a total of 120 supervisors and front-line employees.

Judy was seeing me about her tendency to be controlling. I assigned Judy the job of trying in the period between two coaching sessions to sort out her operating strategy. She came to her next session with nothing to report.

"I couldn't do it. I don't think I have an operating strategy," she said.

"Well, let's see if we can do it together." I pulled out a pencil and paper to make some notes and encouraged Judy to do the same. "Okay," I said, "let me ask you a few questions. When you are at a meeting with the managers who report to you, what are you usually thinking about?"

"Whatever they are talking about is what I'm thinking about. That's what I mean. There does not appear to be any ulterior motive involved. I listen carefully for whatever the issue is and then I encourage dialogue about a plan of action."

"So, would you agree that you happen to be task oriented? It sounds that way. You seem to be more focused on the issues at hand than on, for example, how people are feeling."

"Well, it's not like I don't care about people. In fact I usually notice if someone is not onside."

"What do you do when you think someone is not onside?"

"I seek to uncover what's on their mind."

"And then what?"

"Well, I try to be supportive."

"Good. And what if they don't seem to want or agree with your support?"

"That's when I get a little engaged. When people aren't being reasonable, I do tend to get a little aggressive."

"How so?" I could see a door was opening.

"Well, people say I get a little snippy. I don't know where it comes from. It's like there is a real crab apple inside of me."

"And when people say you are controlling, does that relate to the same response?"

"I'm pretty sure my style when I start to take charge of situations is the same as when someone is resisting me. My empathy seems to go out the window."

"Do you get judgmental?"

"Well, I don't like to admit it, but, yes, I suppose I do."

"Okay, let's see what we have here. When you are in a meeting you are pretty focused on the task at hand. Yes?"

"Right."

"Do you have any sense of what you are checking for in addition to how the task is going?"

"I guess it's something like, 'Are these people onside?'"

"And when you judge that they are not?"

"Then I get aggressive."

"And what does aggression show up as?"

"Sarcasm. I get sarcastic."

"Can you give me an example?"

"Okay. Last week Mary, the girl on my team who leads the retailer complaint department, received another complaint about her team from one of her peers at a meeting of my deputies. She heard the complaint—it was about how her team keeps people on hold for longer than the thirty-second policy—and she got defensive. I felt that she was being a bit of a victim. So I pointed it out. I said I thought she was giving excuses and she wouldn't actually confront the issue until she recognized that it was a problem. I said something like, 'Well, with that point of view it sounds like your team is ready for the technical services department.' It was a snippy thing to say, and I regretted it as soon as it came out of my mouth."

Judy and I managed to summarize her operating strategy shortly thereafter. It goes like this:

- I watch for whether people are onside.

- If I judge that they are not onside, I use various forms of aggression such as sarcasm to get control.

- When they are under control, I feel safe.

Judy had a pretty normal reaction to getting her operating strategy clearly defined. After saying, "yup, that's me," she admitted to feeling a little embarrassed.

"I wanted to think my strategy was something a little nobler than that. I acknowledge that it's true, but it's a little humiliating. Is that all I am?"

"No, Judy," I said. "You are much more than that. Your operating strategy is only one key line of thinking that goes through your head when you are on the job. But it is part of your thinking. And when things are in fact quite onside with your direction, you don't stop listening. You deal with things, of course. You are also, well, Judy. You have your job, your family, your compassion, your interests. But you do have this little routine."

Finding out her operating strategy was just the start of our relationship. We used the concept only to get focused on what triggered her to behave in the problematic way. The larger challenge was to locate the feelings that accompanied her aggressive, sarcastic responses.

But knowledge of her operating strategy helped Judy to self-observe while back on the job. It got to the point where she could actually predict her programmed response and then actually observe herself becoming sarcastic. She reported that she was amazed by this process of witnessing herself. "It's like there is a little me standing on my shoulder watching the other me go at it."

Judy is also a good example of what can be done after an operating strategy is defined. Our next challenge was to get her to be nonjudgmental of her own behavior. As indicated, her first response to discovering her operating strategy was to judge herself unfavorably. My job was to get her to stop judging the operation of her operating strategy. She had to become a nonbiased observer of herself. When she let go of the bias against her aggression, she was able to gain greater control of herself.

The next challenge was to get Judy to be less judgmental of the allegedly noncompliant employees. This involved helping her to connect with what was going on in her head when she was hearing resistance in others. Over time she became aware of her true feelings. When people didn't satisfy her criteria for how one ought to behave, she felt that her own success was at risk. And her success had a lot of baggage attached to it. Judy had a lifelong competition with her siblings for her parents' love. When she sensed that she might not be succeeding at gaining someone's affection, she wheeled out the sarcasm, just as she had done when she was a kid.

This analysis of Judy started with the simple definition of her operating strategy. It was a great way to direct her attention to what goes on in her head when she was triggered. It was an entry into her thoughts and beliefs. It brought forth feelings of humiliation—therapeutic humiliation, if there is such a thing—the feeling of embarrassment over the transparency of her behavior. However sad she may have been to discover her operating strategy, the discovery did shine a light on how and why her meta-thoughts got her into trouble.

Another way to get at your operating strategy is to ask yourself these three questions:

1. What thing do I frequently complain about?
2. What payback do I get from making that complaint?
3. What price do I pay for that complaint?

These three questions won't instantly define your operating strategy, but they might get you moving if you find yourself stuck.

If I had taken this route with Judy, she would have arrived at the same conclusions. She would have identified people not doing things professionally—and as they were instructed to do—as what she frequently complained about. As for what payback she probably got from this complaint, she would have reported that she got people's respect. Her answer to the price question would have been that she sometimes had problematic relationships. From these three questions she would have arrived at how her operating strategy is to check whether the complaint was about to arise yet again, and, if she judges that things are off the rails, become aggressive to get them back under control. By so doing, she would make people sometimes dislike her. But her motive to feel validated was satisfied.

There is no reason to believe that you must work to add to or change your operating strategy. Sometimes just knowing what it is empowers you to override it if you choose. That freedom grants you huge potential. For example, an attention-seeker I know concluded that his operating strategy was to check whether he was loved. When he judged that he was not, he would seek to win people over. Even after he learned of this approach, he was inclined to keep it.

"Sure," he said to a customer of his, "I am looking for your love and respect—that's how I operate. It makes me feel whole. It makes me the lovable guy that I am." His customer liked the full exposure and the kind of sweetness that went with it.

In a sense there is clearly nothing profound about operating strategies. The notion that people move toward security and away from feelings of insecurity explains it quite simply. In fact there is a generic operating strategy whose logic dictates the flow of all the individual versions. The difference between one person's operating strategy and that of another relates to each person's beliefs about what exactly makes the difference between feeling okay and not feeling okay. The generic version goes like this:

> I check whether things are leading to my security and if I don't feel that they are, then I do what usually works for me to either get them on track, or avoid the matter entirely. I do these things so that I can feel whole.

In another sense, in as much as an operating strategy is one more example of an artificial construct created by a lifetime of meta-level thinking, labeling it is a profound opportunity to rise above the judgment game and, paradoxically, to stay down to earth at the object-level. Recognition can make all the difference.

Transcending Your Operating Strategy

I have learned from the writings of Ken Wilber, a philosopher and theorist of consciousness, that there are three main phases to most elevations in consciousness. They make perfect sense and they tend to point to the exact value of learning your operating strategy.

■ *The first phase is defined by your being identified with a certain perspective.* That is, in the same way that you become identified with your feelings—you feel as if the feeling has overtaken you, that you are the feeling—you become one with your point of view.

■ *The second phase is when you disidentify from that perspective.* You realize that you have been identified with your view and on realizing it, suddenly free yourself from it. That's the nature of our three-dimensional consciousness. When we observe ourselves, we become the subject, the observer. The thing we observe becomes the object. Before we reach this point, when we are identified, there is no real split between subject and object. But when we observe, the magic of disidentification occurs.

■ *The third phase involves integrating the two perspectives.* We amalgamate what we like about the first one with the wisdom that comes from being the observer. For example, the attention-seeker, busy seeking attention, is identified with the action of seeking attention. It is who he is. He knows nothing different. When he becomes aware that this is what he tends to do, he disidentifies. He is an observer of himself. He suddenly knows better and realizes that he is, at times, disruptive and overly consuming of others' time. Knowing the difference, he continues to periodically seek attention, but he is more selective.

When you learn your operating strategy, you suddenly become able to reject it, if you choose. Or, you may just go with your traditional operating strategy anyway. But you do know the difference. By defining it, you objectify it. You are no longer lost in your operating strategy. You merely have an operating strategy. You have transcended the robotic programming and you have choice.

There is a real you in there somewhere, someone who doesn't necessarily become burdened with a narrow operating strategy, someone who is not driven by uncontrolled ego responses or driven to develop a false self whose behavior is a response to childhood feelings of comply or suffer. This is not to say that there is a real self. No, we have already eliminated that possibility. But there is an object-focused, nonjudgmental, compassionate person with interests and skills who is free. By freeing yourself of your robotic responses, you become open to the possibility of unbounded authenticity.

CHAPTER 12

A Case of Disidentification

The six types described in this book respond to the facts in front of them in ways that sometimes get them into one kind of trouble or another. The routine meta-level interpretations inherent in their operating strategies trigger feelings of insecurity or cravings for greater security. Like all of us, they unconsciously check whether things are leading to a greater sense of security. If they are not, then their problematic patterns are triggered. In this chapter we are going to look at how emotions are involved in these patterns, and how to handle them. But first, here's an overview of how emotions affect our six types:

■ *The worrier,* confronting certain unanswered questions, experiences fear. Fear drives rumination.

■ *The controller,* feeling a little insecure that things might not go the way she thinks is best, gets very focused; maybe even angry. Her intensity shouts, "Oh my god, we must keep the train on the rails!" Beneath the intensity is a fear of whatever consequences represent that person's worst nightmare.

■ *The fake* projects what he thinks is his optimal image, out of fear that he may not measure up. Sometimes he feels conflicted when he compares the image with the truth.

■ *The attention-seeker* works hard to wave his personal flag. Underneath the effort is a core fear that he will not be seen.

■ *The victim* carries a fear of being responsible for failure. She works hard to avoid culpability.

■ *The prisoner* is hooked by feelings such as anger, rejection, or fear.

Meta-level judgments create emotional responses. For some of us, negative emotions represent a greater percentage of our motivations and behaviors than we would like. So let's look at emotions in order to control them rather than be controlled by them.

Emotions

The word *emotion* can be traced to the Latin word *motere*, meaning "to set in motion" or "to stir." Thus, emotion implies action. Even sadness brings about the action of pulling back from circumstances. It is about buying time to stay safe while the mind processes some kind of loss. Indeed, when we get emotional we are motivated. That's why our employers want us to embrace a mission; they want us to be excited by it so that we move on it and make it happen.

I have learned from the work of the great American philosopher and psychologist William James that a great way to observe the effect of emotion on your motivation is to observe what goes through your mind when you wake up without the aid of an alarm clock from a full night's sleep. Try it. You will notice that the topic that immediately precedes your getting out of bed is usually the one with which you have some emotional connection. When I woke up this morning, I knew I didn't have to get up right away and I began to think about a whole array of topics. I thought about having to go to the hardware store for lightbulbs; I thought about why I lost last night's game of chess; I had a bunch of thoughts about money-related issues; I remembered I needed batteries for a flashlight for an upcoming canoe trip; I thought about this chapter and how I had to include the concept that just because emotions are often about artificial constructs, that doesn't mean they don't have to be processed— and then, wham, I was out of bed. Lightbulbs, batteries, and trips to the bank could wait: I wanted to get to my computer. Scientists have different views on which emotions are primary. One view is that the main emotions are anger, sadness, fear, enjoyment, love, surprise, disgust, and shame. Each of these has its own variations. For example, under the heading of anger might be frustration. Feelings of rejection might come under the heading of sadness. Sometimes, our feelings are a result of two distinct emotions that have been blended. Joy and fear, for example, perhaps produce guilt.

According to the Transcendence Model, what follows from the meta-level creation of self is the tendency to want and to judge. We judge to see whether our wants are being met, and we emote as a consequence. When we aren't getting what we want, we might experience anger or sadness. When we are, we experience enjoyment. When we project our thoughts to the future, we may dabble in fear.

There are two senses of the word *fear,* and it would be useful to differentiate them now. One sense of the word pertains to a specific thing being feared. For example, if you hate to jump off high diving boards—as I do—and you find yourself standing on one trying to muster the courage to let go, then fear is a good descriptor of your experience. There is a specific thing you are afraid of, and it is staring you in the face. This experience of fear is measurable and can easily be seen to correlate with the thing that evokes it. If I get off the diving board, the fear goes away.

This is not the sense of our use of the word, however. In this book we have been discussing a much more pervasive feeling of fear, a feeling frequently present in the lives of the types of people being discussed. You might call our use of the word *fear* an existential use, as in pertaining to the nature of existence. The suggestion is that many of us walk around feeling a general insecurity that seems very much like fear. It is not specific like the fear of jumping from high places into water. It is more general. The effect, however, is still the same. It is an emotional response to what is being perceived in the world of objects. It is a signal designed to get a response. It is a necessary and good component of our makeup.

Emotions Are Good

Indeed, it is important not to infer that emotions are invalid or not useful because they come from meta-thoughts and meta-thoughts create things independently of the objects of the world—in the same way they create a sense of self.

I am thinking of a friend of mine who is a partner in a successful consulting organization. He is thinking of leaving the partnership. He has a rational line of thinking to support his decision. But he feels reluctant to do it because, regardless of his good reasons, he feels connected to his partners. A bond has been built, and just sloughing off that bond because he has good reasons to is not so easy for him.

Now, what help would the Transcendence Model offer my friend? It would say that his feeling of connection is an artificial construct. After all, there is nothing tangible about his sense of dedication. These are just feelings we're talking about. But the model does not prescribe that this ghost called "feeling dedicated to and bonded with these partners" should be ignored. Instead, the feeling must be honored and processed. Ultimately my friend chose to leave the partnership, but only after working through his feelings on the matter. His feelings alerted him to be thoughtful; as a result, though he did what his rational mind told him, his exit was executed compassionately.

Similarly, a prisoner of anxiety can't just say, "Well, this thing I'm fretting over is just an illusion, an artificial construct, so I hereby let it go." It is not really possible to let it go. In fact, as we have said, the way to be free of angst is to move through it, not away from it.

It's also important not to assume that you must adopt the mission to process all the feelings you have simply because of some kind of moral "ought." You may conclude this, if you wish, and it would do you no harm. It might even be a good habit to start. But that is not the point. What we are considering together in this book is how to move past troublesome patterns in your emotional responses—specifically the patterns inherent in the six types we have been discussing. The reason to process feelings comes from your desire to have better control of a problematic pattern in your thinking. Perhaps you are tired of the pattern. Maybe you have found yourself unable to think clearly when you are engaged by your pattern. Maybe you are unable to reach your personal goals because of your pattern. Processing feelings and patterns in your feelings is a matter of personal choice.

We have been talking, so far, about two tools you can use to gradually choose not to go with your programmed emotional responses.

1. One tool is *recognizing how you are triggered.* We explored that tool in the previous chapter by defining our operating strategies.

2. The other tool to help you deal with your patterns is *addressing the emotional issues that pertain to the pattern.*

There are two aspects to this second tool: (1) your general emotional outlook, and (2) the emotional consequences once your patterned response has been evoked. You can use the latter to explore the former. For example, you can explore your tendency to control, and the feelings you have as you attempt to gain control, as a means of locating the antecedent fear that drives the need for control.

Both of these tools—knowing your trigger-response pattern and knowing the emotions that precede and follow from the pattern—will help you enhance your awareness significantly. In turn, your enhanced awareness will allow you, over time, to preempt getting hooked in the first place. When you can catch yourself before getting hooked and actually make choices on the spot that ultimately allow you to bypass getting hooked, then you have made great progress.

But for mastery over your emotional responses, you need more than just awareness of what triggers you, and the emotions you experience. You also need to process your feelings effectively. You have to feel some of the emotion you are attempting to eradicate. You eradicate it by making friends with it. This is where we must now turn our attention.

We Become Our Feelings

When you are struck by an emotion, you experience yourself as that emotion. You lose your sense of self, and your consciousness is occupied instead with the feelings your body is experiencing. We have already discussed that you use the verb *to be* in order to communicate your feelings, as in "I am scared," or "I am mad." Our meta-thoughts have projected our feelings onto our consciousness. We have temporarily set aside our experience of "I am me" and adopted "I am mad" instead.

A client came to my office the other day and declared, "Oh, boy, am I ever stressed out." By the time he left the office, he had shifted to the declaration, "I have stressors." This is a desirable outcome. People need to disidentify from the perspective they have fallen into. They need to regain their sense of perspective.

When my client communicated his feelings of being overwhelmed, I said, "Dave, you're identified with being stressful." "What's that supposed to mean?" was his almost sarcastic reply. I should have known it was dumb of me to throw some theory at the problem. What Dave needed was to experience disidentification rather than have someone attempt to describe it to him for the first time. But now that Dave has experienced it, and we talk about what's on his mind, just reminding him that he has become identified with his feelings helps him to disidentify.

Disidentification is not difficult to replicate. Try it yourself. Think of the last time you were upset by something. Your feelings took over your thoughts. Your sense was not "Here I am experiencing a strong feeling"; it was just strong feeling. In this experience there is a loss of perspective. Strong emotions and egocentric positions (such as pride, anger, and greed) have in common the capacity to cause this loss of perspective.

But the experience of being overwhelmed by a feeling is a kind of bad faith, or a lie one tells to oneself. By becoming focused on one dominant outlook, you deny other truths about yourself. There are, after all, many other truths about you that you are ignoring when you are engrossed in this way: your sense of self, your affection for other people, your history, your pleasures. But you deny yourself cognizance of these things. The idea is to regain your perspective. Later in this chapter we'll consider a variety of ways to accomplish this.

In Dave's case, we simply isolated his dominant feeling and used some psychoimagery techniques to remind him that he could be the observer of his feelings of stress rather than be nothing but the feeler of those feelings of stress. Dave needed to be reminded that he was much more than a stressed-out guy. He was a successful businessman, a father, a husband, a lover of sports cars, and much, much more. Dave had stressors, but he was not his stress.

Isolating Your Feelings

Sometimes it is difficult to locate or define the feelings you are having. For example, the feeling that drives your troublesome patterns on the job may not be readily apparent to you. If you are not hooked at the time of the introspection, you may not have access to the feeling. Or, if you've already been hooked by a feeling, you may not have sufficient perspective to label it.

Everybody's the Same

My own experience is that even when people say they have no feeling, there is probably some subtle thread of feeling in there somewhere. There are physiological reasons to support this claim. For example, as neuroscientist Candice Pert argues, emotions can be seen as participating in body-wide chemical communication systems. They are not just centered in one part of the brain.

One client, a man who was known by his wife and coworkers to be "without feelings," told me that he applied for a promotion and didn't get it. He was adamant that he didn't care. I asked him if he actually wanted to get the job he applied for. He answered in the affirmative. I asked him why, and he gave several different answers. I did come to believe that he wanted the job. But not getting the job didn't seem to push his buttons. Or so he said.

The Transcendence Model led me to predict that there must be anger in there somewhere because he did want something he could not have. He wanted it strongly. My belief was that this man, when he did not get what he wanted, simply blocked his feelings from his awareness. After a certain amount of questioning, he did indeed acknowledge that he was a little frustrated. The final question had to be put as a matter of logic.

"It seems to me that when someone doesn't get what they want, they feel some amount of regret," I said to him. "After all, if you wanted it, then you had some energy for it. Where did that energy go?"

"Well, sure, I suppose there is an equal and opposite effect."

"Excellent. You know, some people would say that you tend not to look at that equal and opposite effect. What do you think about that?"

"I suppose it's true. I got that from my father. By observing him over the years, I learned to stay with the facts."

"Is there a downside to staying with the facts?"

"It makes my wife mad. My kids make fun of me."

"But is there something you lose out on by just staying with the facts?"

"I don't really think so."

This presented me with a challenge. Here was somebody who I was confident was shielding himself from his anger and feelings of rejection. But he was not aware of any pernicious effects. He seemed to have no interest in locating these feelings. He was seeing me about his leadership communication skills. His employees complained that he was cold. For me, there was an obvious link between the complaints of his people and his not being in touch with his feelings.

In fact, for a while, our focus was on what we agreed to call the "equal and opposite effect" of his wanting what he could not have—for example, the sought-after promotion. At the outset, he was uncomfortable calling the effect "disappointment" or "anger." I helped him with using the emotional words. The terms came into use much later in our relationship, but the emotions were present from the beginning.

Try Being Three Years Old

Sometimes people come to me with convoluted stories of who did what to whom and a panoply of feelings. It's very difficult to dissect what is going on in these circumstances. For example, a woman named Lucy came to me with this story:

"I'm all confused. I was taking a new employee on a tour of the plant. John, one of the unionized employees, came up to me on the tour and started a conversation with me that he knew was inappropriate. He didn't know whom I was taking around, and he should have been more discreet. When I told him to come around my office to discuss the matter, he got a little sarcastic. So I had that tension.

"Then we finished the tour and went back to my office. Willie, another colleague of mine, was there at my desk, talking on the phone. It was very inappropriate. He was surely trying to demonstrate that he had the authority to do so. But everybody knows I need my office for privacy, and it's not fair for them to use it for their own private matters. It is my office. But I was afraid that if I said something to Willie, he would use it against me in my next 360-degree feedback—he was one of the people I chose to provide input. Anyway, I've been upset for days."

When I asked Lucy to clarify her feelings for me, she couldn't put her finger on them. She could only say, "I feel mad at the union. I was humiliated by the power game this guy was playing with me in front of the new employee. I am very angry with Willie because he was playing a power game, too. This place is sick. It makes me wonder whether I should stay in this job. I do get job offers from other places, you know."

When I get convoluted stories with an array of undefined feelings, I ask the person to pretend to be a three-year-old kid. Kids of that age don't have much of a vocabulary. Their analyses are usually simple but accurate. I asked Lucy to play this role for a moment and pretend that she had the shop floor employee and Willie sitting in front of her. "What would you say to them?"

After a short while, this is what Lucy said: "I'm mad."

"Why are you mad, Lucy?"

"They don't respect me."

The job of isolating the feelings was pretty much done at that point. Three-year-old kids are much more insightful about these things than grown-ups! In Lucy's case, we agreed that she had been feeling invalidated at work. In fact, over time we learned how Lucy had felt fundamentally insecure her whole life. With the feeling isolated, its ownership claimed, and lots of learning about the possibility of deriving self-worth from oneself instead of from others, Lucy learned to thrive in her organization.

Ask Jung

When somebody does something that pushes our buttons and we can't quite label why we have been so engaged by it, there is a principle from Jungian psychology that is quite useful. This principle says that if there is a quality in another person that irks us, we probably, in some way, have that same quality but have not accepted it. Think of someone you know who has a trait that really bugs you. Let's say it's that the person talks too much. What quality does that person possess that would explain that trait? You might answer that selfishness is the quality that explains talking too much. Do you have that quality in yourself? If it bothers you when other people possess it, the answer will almost always be "yes."

The principle stems from the notion that we all have the same qualities. When we accept them in ourselves, we tend to accept them in others. When we do not accept them in ourselves, we resent them in others.

A man named Chris reported to a new boss named Bernie. One day Bernie stormed into Chris's office red-faced with anger. He stepped right up to Chris and pointed his finger into his face. Chris's heart was pounding. He was having a fear response. Bernie, with a voice that sounded as tight as a clenched fist, yelled, "If you don't get your people to put zip codes on these lead slips, then I swear I'm going to . . . to . . . I don't know what." Bernie turned and walked out of Chris's office.

Chris was a client who was seeing me for reasons unrelated to the Bernie affair. But he told his story at the start of one of our sessions. After hearing it, I said I expected he felt humiliated by Bernie and perhaps rejected. But he was much more interested in talking about how he hated Bernie. He wanted to leave the company because of his feelings. I kept thinking that Bernie hurt his feelings so much that he wanted to flee. But it turned out that Chris wanted to leave because he had such a problem with Bernie.

"What quality does Bernie have that you dislike the most?" I asked, deciding to experiment with the Jungian principle.

Chris showed a real interest in this question. "Well, he is an uncontrolled, bad man. He can't harness himself."

I reminded myself that Chris seemed a very reserved kind of guy—he seemed like someone who was in control of his feelings. Maybe we were onto something.

"Is it possible, Chris, that you see something in Bernie that you don't like in yourself?"

"No way!" he said firmly. "Not possible."

"Are you ever a bad guy? Do you ever lose control?"

"No!" He was a little defensive now.

"Never?"

"Well, rarely. My father used to be like that, and I promised myself I would never take on that trait."

"And with your kids?"

"That's why I said rarely. Sometimes my kids just get so out of whack, I lose it."

"In the same way Bernie lost it?"

"Yes. I guess so. I hate that trait so much!"

Chris revealed that what he hated about Bernie was something he hated in himself. In effect, he was wanting to leave his job because he saw himself in a mirror when he saw Bernie, and he didn't like the image it projected. Our work together shifted a bit so we could work on his self-forgiveness. He had isolated the feeling of anger he had at himself for losing his temper with his kids and the feeling of fear over the possibility that he would become like his father.

Psychoimagery

Several examples in this book call upon psychoimagery as a tool for isolating feelings. This involves freely bringing images to mind. I learned about it through the work of Roberto Assagioli, the founder of a therapeutic movement called psychosynthesis.

When I employ this method of isolating feelings, I ask that you close your eyes and feel where in your body you experience the feeling you are trying to isolate. Then I ask that you place your hand on that place and apply a little pressure so that you connect the feeling to your body. I then ask you to let a picture come to your mind of an object that represents the feeling. It could be any picture. I've heard people refer to a knife, a golf ball, a tight mass, a cotton ball, a tiny box, a river. I ask for a description of the image, so that you are prompted to invest more time and effort in creating what you are feeling. By creating an image, you are suddenly the observer of the image and no longer identified with the feeling.

Once the image has been described, I ask that you give the image a voice. I might ask, "What does the object want to say?" or, "Get the object to finish this sentence for me, 'I feel . . .'" My experience is that the client will then state the feeling we are attempting to isolate.

Sometimes, rather than asking for any image, I will ask for the image of the client as a child. This is based on the belief that the feeling being isolated would have been felt first in childhood. It may even be an unresolved feeling from childhood. By bringing to mind a picture of yourself in your youth, you may well tap into the unresolved feeling in question. I also ask for the memory that you have of that child with this feeling.

Managing Your Feelings

Okay. You're sitting there. You're experiencing this pervasive sense of insecurity, or fear, or sadness. It's right there. Right in front of you. What do you do now?

You probably already know that you can't just suppress your feelings. They keep coming back. Unfortunately, the desire to suppress them comes from the same place where they are generated: the meta-level of consciousness. The effort to say to yourself, "I hereby push these feelings away," falls on deaf ears. The pusher is the pushee, if you know what I mean. As you'll see, only when the feelings are experienced at the object-level can we move past them.

Sometimes we can buy ourselves some time when feelings rise to the surface. For example, we can change the subject, go for a walk, listen to music, talk with friends. But eventually we're left where we started. Feelings do tend to want to be processed. In fact, some of your current vulnerability to strong, undesirable feelings may stem from previous emotional responses that were not fully processed. That's why people go into psychoanalysis: They have decided to process unresolved feelings usually from some time in their distant past.

There are several ways to process feelings. Sometimes we need to understand intellectually the various perspectives that lead to our emotional reaction. For this we can talk to a friend, therapist, or coach. We can also write in a journal or diary. In this sense, processing is a matter of getting our thinking brain to sort out what led to our emotional center's responses. Or, in other words, we attempt to get an object-level understanding of the meta-level judgments we made.

Another step you can take to help you process your feelings is to experience the emotion more fully. For example, if you're feeling sadness, perhaps a good cry will alleviate some of the pressure. This will not erase historical emotional baggage, but it can lighten the pressure until you are triggered again.

I believe the ideal way of processing feelings is to gain the intellectual understanding of the chain of events and thoughts that led to the emotional response at the same time as you allow yourself to go with the feelings. For example, if someone at the office said or did something that has you feeling empty or angry or hurt, it would be good to explore the feeling by talking about it with someone and by allowing yourself to feel the emotion fully.

Owning Your Feelings

But here's the kicker. If you're upset by something someone did or said, keep in mind that the advice to talk about it with someone does not mean to locate how what that person said or did was wrong. No. It means that you must trace your feelings to some aspect of your past or present that makes you feel that way. So often when we feel wronged by someone, we deal with the emotion by directing accountability for our feelings to that person. Instead, we need to take responsibility for our emotional responses. The act of attributing blame is something that makes the emotion stick rather than dissolve.

In this case, "owning" an emotion means to claim it as yours, as opposed to placing your attention on its cause. The moments invested in externally attributing responsibility for the feeling are not "ownership moments." They do not do much toward resolving the feelings. You can blame somebody else for problematic behavior, but for your discomfort you must blame yourself. When I say you must "claim it as yours," I do not just mean to declare intellectually that you have certain feelings. Rather, you must allow yourself to experience the emotion physically. You must allow the experience of it into your consciousness.

For example, consider Jerry, a partner in a successful business with Bob. Their partnership is in jeopardy because they have become less trusting of each other. Recently one of Jerry's direct reports secretly told him that Bob spoke about Jerry unfavorably at a meeting. Apparently Bob said, "It doesn't matter what Jerry thinks is the reason for this. The facts are the facts and we have to deal with the facts. I'm tired of pussyfooting around." When Jerry heard that Bob said this publicly, he was livid. He told me the story.

"And why are you so mad, Jerry?" I asked.

"Bob should not have done that. It undermines my authority and makes us look like we are not aligned," he answered.

Let's be clear on what is happening here. Jerry is having a strong emotional response and is attributing it to the actions of his partner Bob. Jerry is not saying, "I have a thing about not being respected, so when Bob said this, it really pushed my buttons." Instead, Jerry is attributing his anger to some other cause. He is saying, "Bob did it."

One would think that blaming Bob was logical. Bob said something. Jerry was offended. If Bob hadn't said it, Jerry would not be offended. Simple. Then again, perhaps parents are to blame. By the same logic, if they had not produced this person called Bob, then Jerry would not have been offended on that day by that remark. But that's not the way it works.

Sure, Bob's statement contributed to the problem. But the readiness of Jerry's meta-level to interpret Bob's statement as potentially painful set the stage. If Jerry did not have unfinished business about needing the respect of others, he might not have had his reaction. Bob probably shouldn't have said what he said. It probably was counterproductive for the partnership and for his leadership of the company. But that's not the point. The idea here is that by deflecting responsibility for feelings, we stall our processing of them.

I like to approach interpersonal challenges like this on two distinct levels: the individual level and the relationship level.

At the individual level, as I say to my clients, one is wholly responsible for one's feelings. After all, it's your body. If you are having an array of negative emotional experiences inside your body, you own them. They're yours. Deflecting the blame for them is a rejection of ownership. It puts their resolution in abeyance and can impede personal growth. So, for me, if Jerry is angry, Jerry has a personal problem. In fact, Jerry is smart to process his feelings before addressing the relationship problems.

At the level of the relationship, these two partners do indeed need to sort out their behaviors. Perhaps Bob should not have said what he did. It would be prudent for both parties to have some basic guidelines established for their relationship. So Bob is not free of culpability. But Jerry needs to own his own anger.

If you were to ask Jerry today how he sees what happened, he would explain that he takes responsibility for his feelings, and together he and Bob are responsible for their relationship. Were Bob to speak disparagingly of his partner, Jerry would say, "I don't like my anger reaction and I don't like Bob's behavior." To deal with his anger, he would bring it to mind, isolate it as a feeling—independent of cause—and say, "I have anger inside me. It is mine. Insofar as it informs me (about the need for communication with Bob), I am grateful for it. The fact that I am uncomfortable with it is my problem." Then, accepting his anger, or, more precisely, experiencing the anger, holding onto the experience while observing himself do so, he would feel the anger wane. He would be left with his challenges with Bob, but one of his two problems would have been addressed.

Embracing Your Feelings

Effective coaching dialogues that focus on feeling management reach a point of therapeutic climax right after the client has located, isolated, and owned a specific emotion. It makes for a powerful few minutes when:

- The client's emotion is exposed.

- The client's consciousness is filled with the experience of the emotion.

- The client is aware of what's happening.

- Though feeling the emotion fully, the client feels calm about it.

Each time I observe this process, I have the same reaction. I think to myself, "Now this is beautiful." It is an honor to participate in such a real and prolific moment.

How does this apply to you? The climax starts once you take ownership. Then the situation calls for some finesse. We are not looking here for passive immersion in your feelings. For example, processing feelings of sadness is not about rolling around in a pile of painful muck. That only exaggerates things and promotes victim thinking.

Your Threefold Goal

Your goal is threefold: to fully experience the emotion; to be aware that you are doing it; and, finally, to realize that, for lack of a better phrase, all is well. If you are feeling an undercurrent of insecurity, bring it into the light and feel it. Then say to yourself, "There it is. This feeling is a part of me. It is in my makeup. I fight to keep it away but it always returns. Instead, I must welcome the feeling as a part of me. I can let it wash over me as it wants to. There it is."

This threefold experience is the essence of disidentification. It is like sitting on a park bench watching your children play in the playground. You are loving, nonjudgmental, and accepting that these feelings are yours and they are what they are. The psychologist Piero Ferrucci says we disidentify by observing. Instead of being absorbed by sensations, feelings, desires, and thoughts, we observe them objectively without judging them. He says it calls for an attitude of serene observation. This observation removes the self and certain other meta-level constructs from the picture. The feelings being observed are at the object-level and there is no meta-level judgment going on other than the realization that all is well. You are responding to the feelings without ego. Congratulations, you are home.

Perhaps the real meaning of the phrase "the truth shall set you free" lies in this nonjudgmental acceptance of your humanity. Rather than hiding from or resisting ownership of your pain, or anger, or fear, you embrace it as a part of you.

Just the Feelings, Ma'am

But there is a certain nuance to embracing a feeling that is worth highlighting. It involves the distinction between the object of a certain emotion and the emotion itself. For example, if you are afraid of losing your job and you go about your days with that fear gnawing at you, there are two things to sort out: the fear of losing your job, and fear itself. "Losing your job" is the object of the fear; it is the thing you are afraid of. When we talk about embracing your fear, we refer to the fear itself.

In this case, bringing to mind the fear of job loss, recognizing that you possess fear, holding your experience and your awareness of that fear (without an object), and observing without judgment, you will discover a gradual relieving of intensity. Then you are left not with a fear of job loss, but simply with the possibility of job loss. That is a very powerful distinction. Against undesirable possibilities one is ready to strategize and act. Against something like fear of job loss, one is closer to being a deer caught in the headlights. There is magic in isolating a feeling, such as insecurity, and recognizing it for what it is: insecurity, plain and simple.

The six types described in this book all have an undercurrent of insecurity. In some way, they are prime candidates for embracing that insecurity. In a sense, they walk around the planet with an active, private hypothesis, "I am not okay." When they see evidence, via their operating strategy, that their hypothesis is true, they go into their dysfunction and get trapped. But embracing the insecurity moves them out of the cycle.

■ We want the worrier to say, "Fear is a part of my life. I can feel this fear and I can observe it. Then I find peace."

■ We want the controller to say, "The angst from which I run is a part of my life. I can feel this angst and I can observe it. Then I find peace."

■ We want the fake to say, "My effort to be what I believe I am not comes from the sweetest insecurity of all: that I am not good enough. I can feel this insecurity and I can observe it. Then I find peace."

■ We want the attention-seeker to say, "The child in me who seeks to fill my gap has an innocent craving for security. I can feel this insecurity and I can observe it. Then I find peace."

■ We want the victim to say, "The pain I feel when I am the target of accountability is a part of my life. I can feel this pain and I can observe it. Then I find peace."

■ We want the prisoner to say, "The angst that periodically settles in my consciousness is a part of my life. I can feel this angst and I can observe it. Then I find peace."

In each case, the idea is to become the observer of your feelings. But you must be nonjudgmental about the observation; otherwise too many meta-level thoughts become engaged, and they are what stimulated the feelings in the first place. By knowing that your meta-level—as beautiful a function as it is, being the source of your recognition of self, beauty, goodness, passion—is the source of undesirable emotionality; by knowing that the meta-level creates what we have called ghosts; by knowing how this meta-level operates to create your problematic, periodic angst; and by isolating, owning, and accepting the angst, you transcend the robotic machinations of your emotional life and open the door to personal empowerment. You become the manager of your being.

CHAPTER 13

There Goes the Judge

We have seen how our meta-level judgments cause our emotional responses. Our brains are ever so ready to detect what might make us insecure. And we have seen how our troublesome emotional responses can be better managed, first by seeing them for the artificial constructs that they are, and second by specifically isolating and processing them when they strike. Now it is time to discuss how we can manage our judgments while they are happening. Managing our judgments, as we will see, decreases conflict and opens the door to personal freedom.

What does it feel like to have meta-level activity going on in our heads? It's actually an easy question to answer, since usually we are more conscious of our meta-level thoughts than our object-level ones. The direct experience of the facts of the world, without the meta-level activity going on, is a target human experience, as opposed to a common one. Very rarely do we simply concentrate on what we are doing. We are busy having other thoughts.

Those thoughts are given different labels by different people. Shad Helmstetter, a writer in the field of personal growth, refers to them as "self-talk." He says we are busy talking to ourselves in our heads and that this self-talk leads to our attitudes or outlook about things. He suggests that self-talk can be managed and, as a consequence, our outlook can be managed.

I prefer the term *chatter* to self-talk, because it bypasses the use of the word *self*. Self-talk implies that there is a self in there doing the talking, whereas I believe the experience of self is a *result* of the chatter. More specifically, I believe that the voice in your head is the activity of your meta-level thinking. When you are engaged at the object-level, consciousness is not experienced as internal chatter. It is simply consumed by the experience itself.

Try this great way to detect your own chatter. Stop reading for a minute at the end of the next sentence. In fact, I'll join you in this pause while sitting here at my keyboard.

Did you do it? I did. What were your thoughts during that minute? Here are mine:

I should stop writing soon because Dave is picking me up to go for lunch. I need to talk to him. I am concerned that he is not happy. I don't want to keep him waiting. I love Joan (my wife). I hated declining her invitation for lunch. I hope I didn't offend Amy earlier today. Wow, today is a day of possible offenses.

I experienced other mental events, but I wouldn't call them chatter. They weren't sentences or phrases in my head. They simply came to mind. I was aware of them, but I was not aware that I was aware. For example, I heard the main door of my office open and then the sound of two of my colleagues greeting each other. That's what brought thoughts of Amy to mind: She was one of the two people.

The idea here is that when things enter your awareness, and you do not have thoughts about them, you just experience them. These are object-level thoughts. But when there are thoughts that are over and above the experience you are having at the moment, these are meta-level constructions.

We don't necessarily want to eliminate meta-level activity. As indicated frequently in this book, it plays a key role in our lives. But sometimes it goes on a frolic of its own, as lawyers might put it, and from the metal-level activity flow our judgments of others and ourselves and inappropriate emotional pain. These judgments also make it difficult for us to interact with others.

Managing the Judge

Carl Rogers, the humanistic psychologist, writes, "Our tendency to evaluate intrudes on communication." This opinion is perfectly aligned with our discussion about the pernicious effects of some meta-level thinking. This "tendency to evaluate" is what I am calling the tendency to chatter.

We need to consider the impact of chatter on our communications in our exploration of the six types for two reasons. The first reason is pretty obvious: Our relationships with coworkers are the primary source of what pushes us into our troublesome patterned responses. If we can get better control of the judgments that ensue from our dialogues, we are less likely to be provoked.

The second reason is more subtle and profound: When we stop judging people in conversation, we open the door for more authentic and fulfilling interactions. Certainly, our judgments of behavior are critical for effective functioning, but judgments of people themselves erect walls between us and them. And unfortunately, some of us allow our judgments of behavior to bleed into our view of the humans whose behavior we judge. When people pick up on this broad-stroke assessment of their humanity, they disconnect from us. They fear us, and they dislike us. When we find unconditional appreciation of their humanity, however, they bond with us. Aside from the absolute benefit to society as a whole and to the quality of our lives as individuals, this bonding also happens to offer a simple, tangible benefit: People who bond with us tend to be more cooperative. Becoming skilled at managing our judgments ultimately means there will be fewer unfavorable judgments to make.

If you're like 99 percent of the human race, you find it difficult to manage your judgments of others. After all, your meta-level thinking most frequently gets you into trouble when you are interacting with others. It is during these times that the meta-level is most active. It produces judgments; judgments strengthen the sense of self-as-judge; and the judgments create a distance between us, the other person, and the rest of the world. Our selfishness and our judgments sometimes wreck our ability to experience the present and have peace with others. Let's look at an example.

The following dialogue is between two people: a boss, Janice, and her employee, Marvin. In brackets are the chatter or meta-level thoughts of each person—the stuff the two people would never say out loud.

JANICE: *[Oh, there he is, never at his desk, always socializing.]* *"Marvin, have you got a minute?"*

MARVIN: *[Here she goes, she's going to assign me something or criticize me.]* *"Sure."*

JANICE: *"Have a seat."*

MARVIN: *"Thanks."*

JANICE: *[He always slouches. What a lazy image it projects.] "I read over the first draft of your report and thought overall that it was pretty good." [I hope that's all the schmoozing I'm going to have to do, because the details were sloppy and unprofessional.] "There are a few things I'd like you to go over and clean up a bit."*

MARVIN: *[She is never, ever satisfied. Here she goes again. I can't wait for the weekend. I hope she doesn't expect these changes on Monday. Jane will kill me if I have to work over the weekend.] "Sure, what are they?"*

JANICE: *"You did a good job of keeping the reader at the big-picture message. I mean, your conclusion is perfectly clear. But I think a lot of readers are going to be questioning the data. For example, you summarized the survey results as though they were conclusive, but the sample size was so small that you're just begging for dispute." [And frankly, seventy-three people does not come close to being adequate—it makes me look dumb, and I resent it.]*

MARVIN: *[You little crab apple! This is what I hate about you. You're the one who told me seventy-three was enough!] "I thought you supported using that data, even though the sample was so small."*

JANICE: *"Sure. But I didn't want it positioned as though we thought it was conclusive. I was thinking of it as just another chunk of evidence." [But, of course, you're too stupid to put that kind of distinction in writing.]*

MARVIN: *"So what are you saying?" [You . . . Don't you dare wreck my weekend!]*

JANICE: *"Well, all you have to do is go back over sections like that and temper your claims a bit." [I shouldn't have to do it. It's not my job.]*

Marvin and Janice are both too busy with their judgments, fears, and frustrations to be present in the conversation with any authenticity. The sad thing is that conversations like this go on every day, in every office, and all of them deplete the quality of communication and the quality of life for all concerned.

In a sense, both Janice and Marvin are fueling their sense of self throughout their dialogue. For example, when they pass judgment on each other, they are reinforcing their sense of being right and the other person being wrong. And their selfishness intrudes on the quality of their relationship and the goal orientation and productivity of their organization. Obviously, these two have a relationship problem—primarily a lack of trust and certainly a lack of openness. And they both think they are right in their opinions. All of the negative emotions that are between them can be traced to the kind of judgments that they make during their conversations. How often do most of us engage in this kind of dialogue? More than we would like to admit.

The Listening Game

Rogers recommends that businesspeople play a listening game designed to stop personal chatter, so that authentic communication can be experienced on the job. As a former trainer and now an executive coach, I have taught, tried, and prescribed a version of Rogers's listening game with great success. The game is a wonderful way to show people how hard it is to listen. It's also an effective way to demonstrate the pervasiveness of chatter.

The game is simple. One person says something. Another person says it back to the first person's satisfaction. We'll look at a couple of other rules, but that's basically it. The interesting thing is that people find the game difficult to play. I encourage you to try it with a colleague or a friend. You will probably be surprised by how helpful it will be.

For our purposes, we'll call one person the speaker and the other the listener. But when you play the game, and you've successfully listened once, switch roles so you get to be a speaker and your partner is challenged to listen. This will keep the game balanced.

The speaker must say something that he or she finds emotionally stimulating. For example: "On my way to work this morning I got stuck in a traffic jam, and I felt really stressed because I was going to be late for a critical meeting." What the speaker says must take about thirty seconds.

After the speaker has communicated the message, the listener starts with the words, "I hear you saying . . ." Rogers likes this opening because it is a present-tense expression. It is not, "I heard you say . . .", which indicates that the statement is over and done with. And it is not, "You're saying . . ." because even though it's a present-tense expression, it is not necessarily true and so neither particularly humble nor particularly accurate.

The speaker does not have to get his statement back verbatim, of course. Instead, the listener must make the speaker feel wholly heard. Accordingly, the listener must detect the points that the speaker seems to care about and give them back. The listener must also avoid importing things that the speaker did not say, which definitely would make the speaker feel unheard.

The listening game is even more difficult when a speaker communicates something disagreeable in some way to the listener. Let's look at an example of the game from a transcript of an actual, recorded listening-game dialogue. It took place in front of a very small group of people in a department that was having communication problems. I, Art, was the facilitator of the dialogue; Maureen was the speaker; and Bob was the listener.

> **MAUREEN:** *"Bob, I resent it when you don't return my voice mails or my e-mails. Sometimes you are slow at it and other times you don't respond at all. It makes me feel like you don't think what I do is important to the organization. It's like what you do every day is way more valuable than whatever I have to say. Like last week when I called you about that customer complaint and I told you how critical it was, you didn't reply. I sent you an e-mail and you still didn't reply. And I got in trouble for it."*

BOB: *"Oh my god. I have no idea what you just said."*

ART: *"Okay, Maureen, say it again for Bob. And Bob, try your best to hear what she has to say, so you can say it back. Maureen, go for it."*

(Maureen gives the same message but with some very minor changes in wording.)

BOB: *"Maureen, I think you said . . ."*

ART: *"Sorry, Bob. I need you to start with, 'I hear you saying . . .'"*

BOB: *"I hear you saying that I'm selfish with my time. But you know, Maureen, we all have more on our plates than we can handle. And I'm sorry, but I can't get the rest of the details back to you."*

ART: *"Maureen, do you feel wholly heard?"*

MAUREEN: *"No!"*

It took another twelve minutes of recorded dialogue for Bob finally to get Maureen to feel wholly heard. Many things went wrong. Let me share two of them with you.

First, in his response above, Bob went into defensive mode. He explained how busy people are. But the listening game is not meant to be an opportunity for defense. It is only to make people feel heard. Defense is a natural ego response—from the meta-level of consciousness—to a perceived attack. A certain amount of self-control is called for to allay that natural response.

Second, even when Bob got all the message details right—at about the halfway point of the twelve-minute exercise—he still did not make Maureen feel wholly heard. She said she couldn't put her finger on the problem, but it seemed that Bob just didn't "get it." Bob had failed to connect with Maureen's feelings on the matter. We had to go back and start from the beginning.

This was a key moment in Bob's education about managing his chatter. He was about to learn that, for at least a moment, he had to actually let Maureen's feelings about the matter into his consciousness. He had to shut off his meta-level-produced selfishness and allow himself to embrace the feelings of another person whom he, in fact, did not really respect. He did not have to agree with Maureen, but he had to connect with her feeling of being invalidated by him.

But an amazing thing happened when Bob mustered the strength. His eyes opened wide with surprise. "Oh," he said. "My selfish attitude kind of invalidates you and you resent it." Maureen, finally feeling wholly heard, said, "Yes, that's it." We all breathed a sigh of relief. Bob looked humbled and said, "I'm so sorry." He later told the group that it may well have been the first time he had ever truly listened to someone. He suggested it was the first time he had ever consciously experienced empathy. "It's hard work!" he said. Everyone laughed.

It is hard work to listen without judgment. As indicated earlier, it is particularly difficult when we are responding to what feels like a personal attack. It is challenging when we are about to hear something that we believe we're going to find unattractive. Employees, for example, don't often hear criticism; they are afraid of it. Wannabe lovers don't hear rejection; they are seeking its opposite. Rogers is right. Our tendency to evaluate does indeed intrude on communication.

But the game is easy for some people under certain conditions. For example, if the speaker is saying something they want to hear, they have little problem depicting it accurately. Similarly, when the speaker is someone we love dearly and someone we have great concern for, such as our own child, then we usually have little difficulty in setting aside our own motives and perspectives and shifting into an other-oriented mode of operating.

Exiling the Judge

The listening game is a great opportunity to practice shutting off your judgments. But now it is time to look at how one actually exits the judgment mode and enters the place of staying focused on the present. Ironically, this process calls for more meta-level work rather than less. To gain control of your judgment usually involves judging yourself to be too judgmental. You must keep your eye on your habitual judgments.

Most people underestimate the pervasiveness of their tendency to judge. They fail to realize that inside most of their chatter is a pattern of extending object-level facts into meta-level generalizations of one sort or another.

A client named Wayne came to me about problems he was experiencing in balancing his goal orientation with his belief that the here and now is the place to be. "Doesn't goal orientation constantly call for judgment and wishing for something that is not here and now?" he asked. "Isn't that in conflict with the experience of the here and now? How do I reconcile these conflicting motivations?"

Wayne was quite stressed about his conflict. In the daytime he would operate very effectively as a capitalist: chasing goals, making decisions about people, and gaining a reputation as a powerful negotiator. At night he would try to live in the present: spending time with his spiritually inclined wife, listening to classical music, and working in his greenhouse tending to his prize-winning roses. He believed that his off-hours lifestyle was far superior to his business hours, but that, for practical reasons, it was not possible for him to incorporate its values into his professional world. Mindfulness, he thought, was in conflict with pursuing success with verve.

I called on a Buddhist principle to help him. I have heard it referred to as "hold both." The idea is that the two lives of this client were not mutually exclusive. They were only in conflict in his mind. Calling on this principle, I asked him, "When you work in your garden, do you have a vision of how you want it to look?"

"Yes," he said.

"Then are you not being goal oriented even while in your garden?"

"Well, I suppose I am."

"And when you see a weed in your garden, do you pluck it out?"

"Yes. I see your point. They are not as different as they appear."

"Perhaps what you are feeling is not so much that the two philosophies are different, but that at work you go so fast that you lose sight of the present. Perhaps you are a little quicker at judging somebody to be a weed that needs to be plucked. Maybe when you negotiate you are a little more one-sided than you actually care to be."

Wayne and I planned to put it to the test. He was to keep a detailed diary over a one-week period. After each business meeting, he would enter into his diary a general overview of what was discussed at the meeting. Then he would go into detail about the kinds of judgments he made during the meeting. We arranged to talk every day of that week. We would review his diary entries and talk about patterns we observed. We would speak for about ten minutes at 10:00 A.M., 2:00 P.M., and 5:00 P.M. each day. The goal was to get to the bottom of his concern about how his behavior at work was in conflict with his values.

Here is one of our telephone dialogues:

"I just got out of a meeting with my IT guy," Wayne told me. "He was reviewing how the recent crashes of our credit card–processing function were the fault of the installation team and how they were working to diagnose the problems and get them fixed."

"And what were you thinking at the time about this guy?"

"Well, that's the famous six million dollar question, isn't it? I was thinking this guy was full of crap. He was the one responsible for the installation team, and he was making it sound like it was not his fault. I have had problems with him before. He tends to get himself into a mess and never owns the mess or gets a sense of closure. It's like he never actually gets complete control over his function. I hate it. To be honest with you, I was visualizing his departure while we were in the middle of the discussion. And this is my point. I would not call that 'here and now' behavior on my part, and this is a perfect example of my issue. I have judged this man to be unsatisfactory for my organization and have decided it's time to pull the plug. On the other hand, I don't feel particularly proud of my compassion level. In fact, I see no room for compassion."

"I guess the question is whether you have sufficient data to reach this conclusion. It sounds like you're frustrated and you see this mess as a part of a pattern. Tell me, have you ever talked to him about how he seems to deflect blame and never quite gets closure?"

"Not in any formal sense. The lack of closure was never a topic of conversation per se, but I have said before that I wanted closure on certain issues."

"Well, before you blow him out the door, it would be good to have that conversation with him. Meanwhile, I think we've got some interesting things to talk about in our next face-to-face. I've made some pretty

detailed notes tracking what you just told me. Why don't we meet tomorrow?"

Our meeting was the perfect opportunity for me to show him how
he had simply lost control of his judgments. By the time we got together,
he was relatively calm again. In fact, he said he was no longer necessarily
going to remove the IT man from his position. His intention was to have
some fairly clear discussions with him about a need for greater closure.
His shift in mood was going to be instructive for him.

I listed for him the six judgments he had made during his frustrating
talk with his employee the day before:

1. This guy is full of crap.
2. He is making it sound like it was not his fault.
3. He tends to get himself into a mess.
4. He never owns the mess.
5. He never offers a sense of closure.
6. He never actually gets complete control over his function.

I asked him which of the six judgments were factual and objective.
We argued for a while, in a friendly kind of way, ultimately concluding
that none of them was particularly fair. For example, we squabbled over
the truth of the statement, "He never actually gets complete control over
his function." That statement was true in the literal sense, but implicit in
it was the claim that he "ought" to get complete control. Wayne was
willing to concede that this probably was not fair.

In fact, a week later he admitted to me that, as a result of further
internal dialogues, he determined that the nature of the application of
information technology in his organization—they were always using one
leading-edge technology or another—was such that closure and control
were not realistic expectations.

Wayne had a good question for me the next time we got together.

"So how do you actually justify going on intuition and moving somebody out when your gut tells you that it's the right thing to do?"

"I guess you let the facts speak to you," I replied. "You watch your
assumptions to make sure they are based on facts. And you make a call,
the same way that you do in your garden. I'm sure there are moments

when you conclude to yourself, standing alone in your greenhouse, that a particular bush needs to be transplanted because you need space or something. You don't conclude this with some uptight perspective. You know, given your goals for the greenhouse, what you want to do, and you do it. It's a matter of being centered, not anxious. Let's face it, when it comes to that IT guy, you were just angry because when the system is down, it costs you money. The anger affected your clarity."

Wayne had lots of work to do in order to master his ability to manage his judgments. We had to look at what provoked his ego on the job. He had to work through some feelings. Over time he got closer and closer to personal mastery so that he was more or less the same man at work and at home.

Gaining Proximity

If a new client told me that she wanted help with her tendency to control, it would do no good for me to say, "Yes, I see. Well, here's the solution: The next time you take control of the situation, do otherwise. Yes, that's it. Stop controlling." The reason that doesn't work is that the person is not "close enough" to the level of awareness required for self-management. I call the "nearness" to the target level of awareness "proximity." The goal is to continually improve the proximity.

The way to gain that proximity is to see the problem from multiple angles and to process the feelings behind it. Let's look at our controller. She has sufficient proximity to her problem to manage it:

- Once she knows that she associates things not going her way with a frightening feeling of being valueless

- Once she knows how she is always checking to see whether things are going her way or not

- Once she knows how she makes this judgment by moving from specific observations to sweeping generalizations

- Once she has processed her fear of being valueless

When that proximity is gained, suddenly the words to oneself, "Don't do that anymore," present an opportunity to stop the troublesome behavior.

It is useful to see how this works in other contexts.

Perhaps you know that you tend to jump to premature conclusions even though you believe in getting all the facts before you judge. You can locate that rational belief and build a personal promotional campaign to market it to your brain. Perhaps you have the habit of judging that people need solutions, but rationally you know that people sometimes just want to be heard. Highlight this latter awareness as the preferred position and make a personal rule about it. I have heard of personal rules like:

- Never answer until you have verified that the question has been heard.

- Everybody wants to feel heard; give them what they want first.

- Start first with their feelings.

- Paraphrase and check for accuracy.

- Relationship first; task second.

Maybe you know, as an attention-seeker, that your operating strategy is to check for an opportunity to wave your personal flag. With enough proximity, you can override this propensity through deliberate effort. For example, one attention-seeker I know catches his impulse to wave his flag and preempts it with the statement, "I love myself already." His handy rule makes him smile instead of using whatever impulsive attention-getting tool he had in mind.

The list of personal supports in making such changes might range from tools as simple as mental notes and promises you make to yourself, to sticky notes posted on your computer monitor, to asking for the moral support of loved ones and colleagues. You can even build the habit of recognizing your successes at the end of each day. It all starts with proximity. A lot of people read self-help books to no avail. They get an inkling of what their problem is, but they don't take that awareness to the finish line. And they do not change. But with proximity comes the promise of real progress. It takes work.

As part of gaining proximity, it helps to know what to look for. Let's

consider the kinds of choices that each of the six types, with enough
proximity to their choices, could make.

1. If you are a worrier, you will tend to interpret bits of data as
signs that possible danger of some sort is ahead. Catch yourself leaping
to conclusions about vulnerability and stop. You know the things you
worry about rarely come to pass. And you know you don't like the feeling
of worry. So choose not to go there. Instead, act on the issues that you
can address and give yourself permission to choose faith over fear.

2. If you are a controller, you will judge that people are not doing
what they should do. Instead of using specific bits of information to justify your judgment, look internally for what assumptions you are making
and recognize them as such. Are things really out of control? Are people
really not capable? Can you not delegate more by being a more effective
communicator? Resist the temptation to go from the specific to the general. Stay with, and address, the specific.

3. If you are a fake, hiding inside an image, realize that it is because
you judge yourself to be unsafe outside that image. The illusion you project is driven by the illusion that you must project it. Take the risk of
exposing yourself. As frightening as it may seem to you, others will actually prefer the real you.

4. If you are an attention-seeker, know that you judge yourself to
be unlovable, and instead of filling that gap with the attention of others,
yell, in your head, "Stop!" Remind yourself that you are okay. You can
be totally accepting of yourself and thereby not rely on the validation of
others. Impress yourself for a change.

5. If you are a victim, catch yourself when you are falling into that
mode and override the pull toward defense. Realize when you behave this
way that you have judged yourself as being vulnerable to the judgments
of others. Choose instead to completely own the present challenge. The
future is in question. Not the past.

6. If you are a prisoner, you have judged somebody or something
to be unfair, harmful, foreboding, or wrong. Step past the chatter in your

head that supports the judgment. Know that it is an illusion you can avoid. Move to change the circumstances so you can make things right.

All of these solutions call for self-awareness and courage. They require that you transcend the circularity of your programmed response and put a stop to the judgments that trigger it. It does call for a meta-level choice. Making that choice is within your grasp. You can build the habit to remind yourself of things you believe in.

Little bits of progress will boost the speed of mastery. When you actually experience the feeling of being nonjudgmental, when you stop leaping over gaps in facts and instead stay in the moment, you discover a very alluring way of being.

Imagine being in a meeting listening to things that normally push your buttons and instead simply staying right down to earth and calmly addressing one issue at a time. Some thoughts and issues you may file away for future consideration outside the meeting. You might even experience in the meeting your traditional programmed response—the onrush of judgments and feelings—but you somehow calmly observe yourself experiencing them. It is as though you are up on a hill looking down at all the goings-on in the busy place below. You are simply an ever-loving, nonjudgmental observer. You are observing yourself and the other people in the room. To you, things are unfolding as they should. Given all that has been communicated to date, there are no surprises. Whatever comes next is a function of the nature of the communication among all these players, you included. There are no surprises. No bad news. No judgments. The future—a good one—lies ahead of you.

CHAPTER 14

A Way of Being

The word *power* seems overused by the writers of traditional self-help books to refer to the effect of transcending habitual responses to daily stimuli. They believe that when we respond routinely to the various events of our day, we are behaving like robots. But when we override our habitual responses, we are in a position to take full advantage of our freedom as humans. We find, they say, "personal power." This reference to power has always troubled me. It has seemed both trite and inaccurate. Surely there is no newfound energy source, like electricity or steam power, inside those moments of choice.

But I am tempted to use the word myself as I coach people in the practical business world, ready to describe the effects of allaying their habits around judging. Looking up *power* in the dictionary, I see that the word can pertain to a strength or force capable of being exerted. I bite my lip and think to myself, "I'll take it." However, I want a more nuanced sense to the word. So here's my multipart claim:

- When you recognize that you usually respond habitually to situations, and that those responses are based on circuits in your brain attempting to move you toward security and away from insecurity

- And when you have made friends with your fear or experience of insecurity

- And when, at certain moments, you successfully attempt to step outside of those habits

- *Then* you experience several outstanding benefits, which, just this once, I would describe as "powerful."

These benefits include authenticity, a strong sense of will, the ability to put will into action, and the capacity for complete commitment. In this chapter we explore each of these benefits. I presume you have done the work that will open the door to these benefits and that you have gained sufficient proximity. It is time to taste the results of your efforts.

Using the word *powerful* may indeed be appropriate, since we are talking about asserting a strength or force. That's what it means to rid yourself, in a particular moment, of programmed responses. You become a cause agent, capable of having an impact on the world around you.

Authenticity

I have already indicated that I operate on the assumption that there is no self, as some invisible entity inside your body that exists independently of the body. What we sense to be self is a projection of our own mind as it creates a singularity out of the diversity of our moment-by-moment experience. But this does not mean that there is not a real you. What it means is that if you direct your attention to what is in front of you, instead of to yourself or to your judgments, you will behave authentically.

Clearly there is a paradox here. For authenticity to rise, we have to let go of what we think we should be and risk being left with nothing. That nothingness is a fountain of self-expression. We typically fear that nothingness. But we must move toward the object of our fear.

Let's look for a moment at the difference between responding to some matter authentically and responding robotically.

The big difference is that authenticity is without ego. Ego, if you recall, has the job of moving you from a place of perceived potential insecurity to one of suspected greater security. It may be wrong about its perceptions and suspicions, but it is a handy propensity just the same. For example, if you experienced a great deal of rejection when you were young, perhaps you learned to be quiet for fear of further rejection. In a meeting, when someone says something that triggers that same fear response, it would be your ego that keeps you quiet. However, were you to find greater authenticity, your ego would no longer play that role in the same circumstance. You might respond to what you are hearing in some way other than silence. Perhaps you would stick up for someone, or calmly explain something, or even assertively ask another person to find a different way to express themselves. You would not necessarily succeed at changing the situation, but your ego would be relaxed and you would not be wrestling with issues of your own insecurity.

Another characteristic of authenticity is spontaneity. Since behaving authentically means not falling back on robotic responses, who knows what might happen? From somewhere deep inside your mind might spring the most creative ideas the world has ever heard. Insight is best tapped when there is no clutter in its way. Self-orientation clutters.

Authenticity does not preclude emotionality. Indeed, not all emotions come from ego. Anger and grief are two of several emotions that can arise without ego. Terrorist acts can evoke both of these responses. They do not necessarily stem from an egocentric sense of personal violation; they might come from an honest reaction on behalf of humanity.

As a coach I can usually tell when a person is being authentic with me. For one thing, there is no defensiveness or effort to show why he or she is free of blame. In fact, an authentic person is even willing to take blame if somebody seems to feel it necessary; her focus, however, is not on locating causes but on figuring out what should be done to address the problems. The authentic person comes across as having an integrated personality. Life's polarities are held in balance: compassion and personal goal orientation, confidence and humility, playfulness and seriousness, lightness and intensity—they all seem to be present at the same time.

When people behave authentically, they tend to speak the truth. This does not mean that they are blunt. As a matter of fact, I would venture to suggest that refined diplomacy is a hallmark of authenticity. Because an authentic person's personality parts are integrated, traits like compassion and consideration are as active as personal opinion. Authenticity inspires trust. People don't have to fear being misled by authentic people. There are no selfish, ulterior motives for them to suspect or grapple with.

Will

When a person has found the way of being as described in this chapter, he is free of day-to-day personal angst. There is no longer the worrier's fear of what unfortunate thing might happen or the controller's concern about losing control. There is no fear of being found out. There is no fear of being left alone, or of being culpable. Instead, there is a sense of strength. In this way of being, there is the ability to let things go. Instead of getting hooked by someone's egocentric jab or provoked by some news that historically would have caused a sense of angst for this person, there is a confidence that one is able to deal with whatever life delivers.

This inner strength manifests itself as will. The word *will*, of course, is the future tense of the verb *to be*. This is worth a moment of reflection. In a sense, when a person who has transcended her robotic ways says what she will do, she is collapsing time. She is not just saying what she will do at a certain time, she is declaring to the universe that as far as she is concerned, her statement declares that she has already incorporated fulfillment of her promise into her being. The sentence, "I will pick up my son at 3:30 P.M.," means a certain little boy can count on the 3:30 arrival of his mother. Period. This is a mother who will keep her word.

One of the biggest issues humanity faces is what I call "forgetting conviction." It is the reason people don't keep their New Year's resolutions, why they don't lose weight when they say they will, or why they start and then stop exercise programs.

I remember myself twenty-five years ago promising to stop smoking. I tried several times before I was actually able to do it. On one cloudy day, I would finish a cigarette and declare to the person next to me, "That's it, I quit." I would put the cigarette out, fully intending, with all the conviction in the world, to quit. But then, sometimes only a half hour after that big production, I would, for example, be driving onto the on-ramp of a local highway—a trigger point for this smoker—and bingo, I would reach for a cigarette. I would remember my intention to quit, but I would forget my conviction.

Nowadays I would say I was not close enough in proximity to the awareness required to actually implement my will. I possessed inadequate control over my meta-level thinking. I was ruled by my meta-level. This was an issue of will. Not in the Victorian sense of willpower, as a force of will that would fight against personal appetites, but in the sense of being able to transcend the struggle between appetites and conscience.

My smoking habits motivated me to reach for cigarettes. My meta-level thoughts surrounding smoking were based on fears that I would die, judgments about why I was wrong to smoke, desires to please those around me, shame at lacking the will to go through with it. At one moment I was a smoker, identified with the pleasure of the whole affair. At another moment, I was a judge, disgusted by my weakness. What I had to learn is that I could be a will.

The work of the founder of psychosynthesis, Roberto Assagioli, stimulated me to take a new direction. For the last twenty years I have successfully operated on the assumption that when you gain control of your meta-level thinking, by knowing what triggers you and by accepting the insecurity underlying all of your psychological machinations, you suddenly become a will.

When we stop being whatever crosses our consciousness, we are left with will. We choose. We act. We observe our judgments and our emotions. The observer is the will. We do not possess any more substance when we are in this form than when we are identified with our feelings of self or our emotions. There is nobody in there, but things are getting done. We experience life in the present while the future is coming at us. Instead of functioning based on our habitual pressures, we function according to our intrinsic nature.

Will in Action

Two sales representatives were hired by a corporate communications firm. They had similar career backgrounds and the exact same university degrees. They had both been very successful in their prior jobs. They were well paid in their new roles. As a matter of fact, they were hired into the roles because they were successful, dynamic heavy hitters.

Their jobs were to sell their employer's very expensive services. The problem was that the world economy was sinking, and the services they had to sell were much less in demand. Both gentlemen started work on the same day and received the same training. Let's call one man Will, and the other Cant.

Unfortunately, after six months on the job, both men had to be let go. They had sold nothing. Their employer could no longer justify its investment in them. The leader of Will and Cant had to sit them down one at a time to discuss termination. Cant was the first person to go into the boss's office for the termination conversation. Here is how he responded:

"This is disgusting. You people hired me with the lure of big money.

I feel misled. The customers are not receptive to our approach; the service offering is not really ready to be in the marketplace. Marketing has not finalized its positioning, let alone properly instituted a supportive advertising campaign. You have not once gone on a sales call with me. This whole affair has been a sham. You'll hear from my lawyer! I'm going to squeeze every last cent out of this rip-off organization. You watch me! Nobody! Nobody wrecks my career like this! You'll pay!"

Cant stormed out of his boss's office, slamming the door behind him. Over the next several weeks he met with two lawyers in order to commence legal proceedings. The first lawyer he judged to be too soft for his needs. The second lawyer, he thought, was sufficiently like a vicious shark to qualify for the job. Cant told all his friends of the way he had been victimized. He spent many an hour bemoaning his losses, in terms of career momentum, legal fees, and embarrassment. He brought his anger into his home. It made his kids cry on more than one occasion and infected his relationship with his wife. Cant was one very angry man.

What about Will? He sat down with his boss and heard the company's decision. He said, "Well, we knew this could happen. The fact is, I did not fulfill my part of the bargain. I understand. It is unfortunate. I'll be fine. It was an interesting experience, wasn't it? Thanks for the education and the honor of working with you."

Will moved on in his life. While Cant was involved in his legal wrangling, Will found work. Ultimately, they both ended up with the same financial settlement. Will accepted the company's initial generous offer, and Cant settled out of court for an amount that was a little higher than Will's, but his legal fees balanced things out.

I spoke at length to the HR executive who oversaw the process of Will's and Cant's exits. We talked about the vast differences between the two men's reactions. Cant responded like an angry victim. He got lost in his reaction. It held him back from productive activity. His ego was fully engaged for weeks. Will, on the other hand, had a realistic view of the circumstances. He was not moved to blame. He dealt with the future coming at him calmly and confidently. He moved on.

My coaching client asked Cant to explain why he was pursuing litigation. He answered, "Because you messed with me." Will's answer for why he did what he did was, "I just moved on. No sense in messing around."

People who recognize meta-level thinking for what it is see themselves as choosers instead of deliberators. The rest operate on the mistaken assumption that in advance of our decisions we go through a rational thinking process in order to define our best choice. There is reason to believe that choices are not really made that way at all. For example, the neuroscientist Benjamin Libet has shown that there is a half-second delay between when our unconscious mind makes its choice and when our conscious mind becomes aware of the choice. We think we are driving the decision bus, but what's going on below the level of our awareness is what really has the control. When most of us have made a choice in life—even a little one like going to a certain restaurant for lunch—we look back after our choice and provide a rationale. But in advance of our choice, we just choose. When we look back and provide our explanation, we are more or less pretending that our conscious mind went through some process of deliberation. When you have become a will, you make choices. They come from deep inside you. You don't pretend there are explanations.

Will lets stuff go. He has the same impulses as the rest of us. We never lose our natural impulses. But Will is will, if you know what I mean. He sees what is going on in his head. But he sees it for what it is. Cant, on the other hand, tends to get lost in his responses. As a matter of fact, in the process of providing him with outplacement support, I learned that his degree of anger came from unprocessed anger from his childhood.

Commitment

In addition to becoming more authentic and willful, another consequence of knowing your operating strategy and processing your feelings is the wonderful effect on the capacity for commitment. Let me tell you about my friend Lou.

Lou and I have been friends for thirty years. One thing we had in common for the first fifteen years or so of our friendship was a fear of commitment to women. Both Lou and I would find new girlfriends, get intimately involved, and then, when the topic of the next logical step would arise, weasel our way out of the relationship. There was even one occasion where we broke up with our respective girlfriends on the same day. We had shared our reluctance to move forward and agreed we would connect later that night, after we had both done the deed.

I am proud to say that with a fair bit of therapy and effort, I managed to leave my fear of commitment behind. I met and married Joan, my cherished wife, more than fifteen years ago. It took Lou a few more years to make the leap into marriage. So for the first part of my marriage to Joan, we would observe Lou bringing one new girlfriend after another to our home for dinner.

One night, Lou was to come for dinner with his girlfriend Nancy. Joan and I were in the kitchen when the doorbell rang. We both went to the front door to welcome our guests. Joan opened the door and there was Lou, alone. I heard her whisper, "Oh, oh." Assuming that Nancy was suddenly out of the picture, I felt sad for her and for Lou. They had seemed like such a fine match.

Lou is a pretty smart fellow. He knew he had a problem. His rationality and realism meant that he could not commit. Yet he wanted to commit. It was a shame. For Lou, the thinking had always gone like this: "How can I ever stand in front of a justice of the peace, or anyone else, for that matter, and declare, 'Nancy, I commit to you for the rest of my life,' when I know that 50 percent of all marriages end in divorce? I can't predict the future! I can't commit to what is not in my control."

So Lou went through the years—as had I, since my view had been similar to his—wishing he could commit but feeling conflicted over his rational belief. It felt to him like a matter of integrity.

But Lou surprised us that night. At the dinner table, in Nancy's absence, he raised his glass of wine and said, "You guys, I want to propose a toast." Always eager for another sip of a good Amarone, I raised my glass, wondering what Lou was about to say.

"Nancy and I are engaged to be married. Here's to our future!"

"Lou-baby!" I yelled. "Congratulations!"

The three of us chattered away for the rest of the meal. After we cleaned up, Lou and I went for a walk. We walked the streets of my neighborhood, smoking a couple of big stogies.

"Lou, my friend, how did you do it?" I asked.

"Well, it's true. Nancy and I are committed. So long as neither of us changes as people, and so long as we are faithful to each other—well, this is it. Permanent."

I squinted my eyes—not from the smoke of the fat, smelly cigar but from what I sensed, logically, was a bypassing of the fundamental problem. Lou had given himself an out. He was not committed, no matter what. He had conditions to his commitment. He had still not actually made the leap. Standing out there on the diving board of life, he could not make the jump.

Commitment calls for a no-holds-barred approach to things. The meta-level gets in the way. Our fears prevent the jump. There may be all sorts of logic behind the fear, but it is just retrospective rationalization. The fear comes first and rules. Until we put the meta-level in its place, our capacity to choose will always be its victim. But when we have done the work, we become authentic, willful, and able to commit.

My impression is that marriages that start with prenuptial agreements may be rational but don't last as long. Business commitments made with exit clauses aren't true commitments. When a sales leader says, "We're aiming for a 20-percent increase," there is something fishy going on. As soon as we visualize what might excuse us, we let ourselves off the hook.

Humans normalize things very quickly. When we say, "I'll just skip this exercise session, since I'm feeling particularly tired today," we set the stage for subsequent excuse giving. When we tell ourselves at the start of an extramarital affair, "Surely a two-second kiss on the lips is forgivable," we're no doubt on the path to an exciting but inevitably painful future. Failure is assured the moment we say, "I'll smoke this one cigarette, and then quit later." We usually feel a little funny about letting ourselves down in these ways. But after a few permissions, we're on our way. We normalize things that were once not really okay.

Strangely, normalizing has a good side to it. The speed at which people normalize things reflects the speed of learning. We do something a few times and we learn it. It works for the good things and for the bad. Our brains stop registering things if our meta-level thoughts deem them unnecessary. We have to manage the amount of stuff that makes it to consciousness because we just have too much going on.

An interesting problem is that my friend Lou and other commitment-phobes and wannabe exercisers and smoking-quitters have what looks like a very convincing argument at their disposal: reality. Surely one more smoke will do no harm. And maybe a little kiss, in the big scheme of things, does have very little meaning. What's wrong with a little reality?

When people let their meta-level thoughts rule, identifying with all the reasons they can muster for being the legitimate excuse giver, they deny themselves the chance to become pure will. They do not fully commit.

Now that my friend Lou has three kids, I do believe he has totally reconciled himself with the possibility of total commitment. If today you ask him about commitment and how he handles the fact that half of marriage commitments fail, he will say that the problem rests in the passage of time. He would say, "Look, commitment is about being—not time! When I commit, it is for eternity. And what if the conditions change? Well, right now, with all my being, I am 100 percent committed to Nancy. The future does not exist. Talking about future conditions is not something I spend time on. Not interested."

Lou, in my opinion, is clear.

The effects of this kind of position on commitment are many. First, people of total commitment live by their word. They do not lie to themselves about their intentions. They have cleared away all of the chatter in their heads, and they simply mean what they say. They spend no time allocating blame, because, for them, blame does not exist. Commitment and fulfillment exist. When something goes wrong, they move to fix it. Action is the name of the game.

If they are on a team, they are committed to the performance of the team and to their role on it. If someone on their team has a problem, they are there to support the person and the team. If they are confronted with no-win scenarios in their team challenge, they move to overcome the obstacles just the same. They don't divvy-up responsibility, saying, "Billie has 20 percent of the job, and Linda has 50 percent of the job and I have this 30 percent over here." They say, "I am focused over here and have total accountability for my area of focus. And, Billie, Linda, and I all have total accountability for the whole thing."

People who have transcended the meta-level dynamics of their minds have the same fears as the rest of us. But they don't fight these fears. They embrace them and act on them as necessary.

- They don't get lost in worry. They choose faith. They will succeed. They know it.

- They don't fall into a neurotic quest for control. They see what must be done. They delegate. The future is coming at them, and they efficiently make things right. They do not fill with angst, because angst does no good. They roll with the punches, stay focused on the goal, keep in touch with their compassion, and calmly lead situations to success.

- They don't hide in a false projection. They expose themselves with nothing to hide. They are okay as they are.

- They don't seek attention. They don't suffer from their emptiness. They accept it. They have infused their acceptance of it into their being.

- They don't spend time on blame. They simply take responsibility and act.

- They don't find themselves prisoners of anxiety; their fears move through them, and they observe their fears while they act on their crazy world.

The problems most of us have on the job can be linked to inner fears. A sales rep in one company is afraid of picking up the phone. It hurts so much to be rejected! A manager in another company is afraid of confrontation. She thinks there is nothing worse than being unloved. An accounting clerk in the office down the hall doesn't like speaking up at meetings. She is afraid she'll say something stupid.

But when we understand our fears and process them, they dissolve. When we comprehend this dynamic that operates in our heads, we transcend it and find ourselves making choices, being wholly committed, being authentic. When people are focused on the object-level, they act within it, losing themselves and finding freedom.

CHAPTER 15

A Better Way

In the world of corporate training from which I hail, "sustainment of learning" is one of the profoundest of issues. So often people walk into a training session, learn new things, say, "Yes, yes, that was very interesting," and then never incorporate the new information or methodologies into their jobs. The problem stems from what I referred to in Chapter 14 as "forgetting conviction." People have an exciting moment or two, take on some degree of conviction that they will indeed use the new discovery, and then exit the session, forgetting all about it.

To help you sustain the increased awareness you have gained by reading this book, I would like to recommend some guidelines. Obviously the message of this book is that it is going to take some work on your part to leave your troublesome behaviors or responses behind as you grow and make changes in your life. The Transcendence Model and the distinction between the object-level and meta-level will be very helpful in this regard. But there are two practical steps you can take as you move forward:

1. The first step is to use pencil and paper in learning to uncover your operating strategy. This will help you isolate what is triggering your behavior. At the end of each workday for a week or two, record what was going on around you that day when you fell into the troublesome behavior. Watch for patterns. For example, did your buttons get pressed because someone disagreed with you? Did you hear certain news that engaged a worry or an attention-seeking program? See if you can label the trigger and the response.

As you will recall from the discussion of your operating strategy in Chapter 11, in addition to labeling the trigger and response pattern, you can trace the judgments in your head that lead to the response. For example, if things in your office go awry and you find yourself jumping into defense mode, try to unravel the thoughts that led to the feelings. You might say, "Hmm, Mr. Jones found out that the document went out late. I began to think of how it wasn't my fault. I guess I was afraid he was going to blame me. That would mean I am less secure in my job. I am afraid of losing my job. I am afraid of my world falling apart. That's it. That hurts." As a result of that thinking, you may conclude that your operating strategy is to keep an eye out for whether you'll be blamed, and, if you judge that you might be, then, out of an experience of fear that your world will fall apart, to equip yourself with a defense.

2. This prepares you for the second step you can take to ensure sustainment. It could require several hours of your time, broken up into smaller chunks, dedicated to processing the feelings that drive and result from your operating strategy. It also calls for a certain amount of courage. It is understandable that you would want to veer away from the emotional work. Negative emotions, after all, are there to signal that something should be avoided. We are programmed to avoid those feelings. The chapter on emotions (Chapter 12) addressed how you can process them anyway.

Beyond these two practical steps, there are other things you can do that are not necessarily time consuming and that will improve the value you will get from this book. They pertain to:

■ *Full-Exposure Communication*: how you can communicate with others free from unwanted meta-games

■ *Flow*: how you can approach certain tasks so that you are as close to the truth you as you can get

■ *Meditation*: how you can tap your insight through various meditative tools

Full-Exposure Communication

A week ago someone in my office came to me to talk about a project we were working on. Unfortunately, two dynamics were in conflict during part of our conversation. There was the topic being discussed, and then there was an unspoken agenda item. My colleague was asking me questions about how I wanted the project to proceed. What he wasn't telling me was that he had already engaged in contradictory dialogues with other members of our team. I won't bore you with the details, because this kind of game playing is rampant in business and I'm sure you know all about it. However, what I do want to do is show you how full disclosure can help keep you and the other business types discussed in this book out of trouble.

But first let's look at *partial* disclosure communication. The problem with this approach is that it involves a communicator avoiding various truths, including the truths that generalizations are not rational and that things like blame are illusions. This style of covert thinking is antithetical to what we have been discussing throughout this book. For example:

- *Worriers* who only partially disclose their fears to someone are only going to find their worry increasing.

- When *controllers* engage in partial disclosure, they spark mistrust in their listeners; in turn this mistrust signals weakness to controllers and increases their sense that they need to control.

- *Fakes* are partial communicators by definition. The more they participate in this form of communication, the worse their symptoms.

- One thing *attention-seekers* do not want to draw attention to is their ulterior motives. This would reveal their insecurity. Partial disclosure communication only serves to drive them deeper into their behavior.

- Partial disclosure is tailor-made for *victims*. By hiding their fear of being blamed, they are nourishing an illusion.

- *Prisoners* need, more than anything else, to unlock the things that are bugging them. Partial disclosure keeps these things in.

In contrast, full exposure communication requires you to:

- Expose your vulnerabilities.

- Stay focused on the facts and avoid generalizations.

- Realize that if it's bugging you, it's your problem.

- State your hidden opinions.

Let's look at these one at a time.

Expose Your Vulnerabilities

When you go into a conversation feeling insecure, say so. What I wished my colleague had said to me last week was that he was disinclined to do a certain job because he was afraid of the effect it would have on him personally. Rather than exposing that to me, perhaps out of fear of how it might look to me, he kept it quiet. He just wanted to feel me out on how I might respond to his resistance without actually exposing the resistance.

His choosing to hide his true motivation had several regrettable effects. As I sensed he was holding something back, I began to mistrust him, the first step in what could have become a deteriorating relationship. A second was that by behaving as a fake, hiding things rather than just being honest, he was setting himself up for awkward feelings of guilt for not being open—the stuff of sleepless nights. A third was that by making the circumstance so "political," he was making it difficult for us to get to the bottom of why we were finding it difficult to work together on this project.

As a matter of fact, we did get to the bottom of the problem. I exposed my sense of there being an unspoken undercurrent. He ultimately brought his previously covert mission to the surface. We sorted out a way to address his needs and the company's needs. By pursuing the truth and calling on our mutual respect, we reached a very comfortable plan. If we had not made this progress, then the culture of our team would have been damaged, more private, time-consuming dialogues would have been undertaken, and a bunch of undesirable interpersonal game playing would have been supported.

It's not easy for any of us to expose our vulnerability. That's why we want to keep it hidden. It doesn't feel good. But I remind you that the fear is an artificial construct. It is something produced inside your brain, a real feeling but not a thing-in-the-world phenomenon. And the good news is that finding the courage to expose your fear will almost always work in your favor.

You have to watch that you don't use full-exposure communication as a tool for saying blunt things. The idea is that you are exposing *your* vulnerabilities as opposed to someone else's. I remember once introducing the concept to a team. For a few weeks afterward the team members walked around saying relatively unpleasant things to each other. "Full exposure, I think you did a sloppy job on that report," or "Full exposure, I think that was a dumb thing to say at the meeting this morning." Not quite what I had intended.

But when you are afraid to reveal a personal vulnerability, such as your own fear about some matter, you should look at taking the risk. The way you disclose is key, however.

For example, let's say you have a chance for a promotion. How you position yourself in your boss's eyes is critical to getting that promotion. You think you may not be ready for the job, but you can't be sure. You don't want to say, "Boss, I have a fear that in fact I am not ready for the job, but I am a great believer in the importance of exposing my fears, so there you go. What do you say? Can I have the job?"

Disclosing your fear is still the way to go, but you may need to do it with some degree of diplomacy, which may well show your boss that you have humility and honesty. For example, you could say, "I do crave this promotion, and I know I would work like a dog in the role, but I can't help but have some concerns about certain aspects of the role. In fact, I would like to talk about some of them with you. I'm sure we both want to do the right thing."

Go for it! The truth works.

Stay Focused on the Facts and Avoid Generalizations

Another aspect of full-exposure communication calls on a principle we have been discussing throughout this book. In conversation it is important to differentiate between object-level reality and meta-level meanderings. If you blend them, people may get turned off. For example, have a look at the statements below and notice what is real versus what is meta-level. The following statements are from a dialogue I overheard in a client's lunchroom:

"Did you hear that our parent company is defending against a forced takeover by the monster XYZ company? Takeovers are scary. People lose their jobs. And XYZ is known for taking somebody over and moving people out. Bob would surely be done for then, wouldn't he? He's so inefficient they would probably just eliminate his role and there would be no consequence. Gone and forgotten. He deserves it. Of course, it could happen to any of us, I guess. Only the strong survive, as they say. What I would hate is that we would have to start working at their location rather than our own. I bought my house with my work location in mind. It would really bug me if I had to start driving across town like that. I mean, what about my kids, for heaven's sake! They are settled into school, and have their own friends. It would be terrible! You know, it's all about greed."

Everything in this paragraph looks like it might be factual, but very little if anything in it is about the object-level. The speaker obviously has a lot going on in his head that is generated by meta-level activity. Full exposure does not mean to get out every mental event. It means to distinguish between what's real and what's not. The person above might have said something as simple as, "The possibility of a takeover sure does get my mind racing." This book is about the possibility of seeing those meta-machinations for what they are.

Realize That If It's Bugging You, It's Your Problem

When we do talk to people about the things they do that bother us, we tend to focus on what they did rather than how our buttons have been pressed. Full-exposure communication calls for you to expose how you, and not the other person, are accountable for your feelings. "You hurt my feelings when you said I was lazy" is something I heard one person say to another. Notice how the hurt person is blaming somebody else for her feelings. This, as we have already discussed, is diverting her attention away from her own unresolved feelings. Instead, we must own our anxieties. If it bothers you that you've been labeled "lazy," then apparently you have some unresolved feelings on such matters—after all, some people wouldn't be bothered by it at all. They might implement some simple strategy, but they wouldn't feel particularly threatened.

State Your Hidden Opinions

Just under thirty years ago, I was in an "encounter group." Ten of us assembled weekly in the office of a therapist. The group met for over a year. We talked openly about our problems. I was there as part of the process of learning to become a therapist, but I was no less troubled by life than anyone else, including the leader. It was a great way to hear honest feedback from people and to learn about humanity.

In these sessions we engaged in true dialogue, and more often than not things got quite heated. I remember one meeting when I asked a woman whether she had really thought through an opinion she had expressed. The leader of the session, a very experienced therapist, stopped our momentum and gave a speech about "bullshit."

"Art," she said, "I get the feeling that your innocent-sounding question is actually hiding an opinion. Why don't you state your opinion?"

"No it's not!" I countered.

Everybody in the room looked at me. I felt like they were all pursing their lips and lowering and shaking their heads as they judged me to be partially exposing.

Feeling somewhat ashamed, I admitted, "Well, maybe I've got an opinion in there, but I don't want to just spit it out until I hear more."

Everybody shook their heads.

"Okay, I'm afraid to give my opinion!"

"What is your opinion?" the original speaker asked.

"My honest opinion is that you rarely think things through," I said, facing the woman. "You are so impulsive. You are driving me crazy!"

I went on for a while. I learned about my own tendency to judge. What I thought was about my scattered, impulsive friend was really about my tendency to judge certain people to be scattered and impulsive and therefore undesirable. What I learned from that little exchange is that my "bullshit" was in having disclosed partially. I wasn't being open. I was blocking the momentum of the relationships in the room, of the dialogue in the room, of my own development as a communicator, and of my friend's development.

This is not to say that business meetings need to be treated as therapeutic encounter groups. It is only to point out that for honest communication to take place—and honest communication is desirable if you're going to transcend the traditional meta-level merry-go-round of judgments and problematic, robotic thinking—then you might work at fully exposing what's going on in your mind. It will keep you honest, in touch with the judgments you have made, and open to the possibility of sustained transcendence.

Flow

Focusing on the object-level instead of on your meta-level thoughts, a constant theme of this book, is another way to sustain what you have learned. You can create the circumstances that make this possible. It means becoming less encumbered by feelings of insecurity, pride, and self-defense, and more likely to experience the joys of being lost operating in the "real world."

We have already talked a bit about the work of the psychologist Mihaly Csikszentmihalyi. He speaks of "psychic entropy," the tendency of consciousness to disintegrate. He also talks about the opposite of this disintegration. He refers to "optimal experience" or what could be called true human happiness. He calls it "flow." If you get immersed in some activity, such as playing golf, building a shelf, delivering a presentation, creating a spreadsheet—then you may well transcend normal existence for a while by, ironically, getting down to earth.

Csikszentmihalyi's concept of flow is very applicable to our jobs. The main conditions required for the experience are that we must have a goal, be challenged, be concentrating on what we are doing, and we must have some of the skills called for in order to achieve the goal. If we are attempting to do something that is too far above our current skill set, then we are not likely to achieve the desired psychological experience. Alternately, if what we are trying to do is quite easy for us, then our mind wanders off our work because we don't really need to concentrate.

But when it works, the effect is profound. First, chatter stops. There is no longer a voice going on in your head that is busy judging, thinking about other things, experiencing a sense of self. There is no ego. There is only the thing being attended to. It is an experience of total immersion.

Action and awareness are one. When it's over, and you look back, you do realize that it was very pleasurable.

In fact, if you stop in your head to look at whether you are having fun, the actual state of transcendence disappears for about the period of time of the reflection. It's that same paradox again. Self intrudes. When it looks for happiness, it is cut off from it. There is no room for ego in happiness. There is only room for being. Is it easy to have this experience? Absolutely! You undoubtedly have already experienced it in your life. In truth, most people I speak to about it have it much more in their private life than they do at work. Yesterday a woman told me she experiences it when she plays tennis. A man recently told me it occurs when he is working on the guts of his race car. Another fellow last week told me he falls into this frame of mind when he works to clean his apartment more quickly than he did the last time.

Sometimes I find myself in such a transcended state while I am coaching someone. I lose myself. I listen carefully, ask questions, make comments, move the dialogue to some next, seemingly healthy place. At other times, I have to admit, I am more preoccupied with my own "stuff." The quality of my work probably goes down a bit, but I don't think it is apparent to the client. Only I know when I'm not operating in harmony with the room.

The real moral of the story here is that when we have labeled our problematic patterns, when we know more about what triggers us, and when we have embraced the emotions that we have been resisting most of our lives, then we are much more able to manage our meta-level thoughts. We can experience life without intrusive chatter. We can find joy. There is joy in doing. It is not in achieving. It is in what any living creature does. It lives.

Meditation

There are dozens of meditation techniques that will effectively give you freedom from meta-level robotic machinations. Two of them appeal to me for their easy access to that freedom and their nondogmatic approach. It's ironic because they both derive from religions that are thousands of years old.

The Buddhist Approach

My experience is that the effect of falling into flow is identical to the experience created when practicing a certain Buddhist meditation. It is about getting involved in the moment. The Buddhist monk Thich Nhat Hanh describes it best, in my opinion. He says we can experience mindfulness by simply repeating to ourselves that we are doing what we are doing. We can evoke the experience at any time. "Sitting at the keyboard, typing, I am aware of sitting at the keyboard typing." Or even, "Breathing in, I am aware of breathing in. Breathing out, I am aware of breathing out." Instead of allowing our attention to float to wherever our mind's meta-level wants to take it, we direct our attention to what we are doing.

This sounds easy, but in fact most of us tend to drift. It sounds perhaps even of low value. After all, what magic can ensue by saying to ourselves that we are doing a certain thing and that we are aware of doing it? Well, it's actually pretty special. Try it, for twenty minutes or so. You'll probably discover yourself forgetting to direct your attention to what you are doing. But when that happens, simply go back to verbalizing (out loud or to yourself) what you are up to and that you are aware that you are up to it. After the twenty minutes there is a great chance you'll notice a favorable effect on the chatter racing in your head and your consequential feeling of centeredness.

Hindu Meditation

I learned to meditate using a mantra—a sound I repeated in my head—when I was nineteen years old. This was meant to be the easy kind of meditation. One doesn't have to try hard to concentrate with a mantra. All one has to do is catch oneself forgetting to repeat the mantra and casually go back to the repetition. You close your eyes, relax, and start repeating the sound, at whatever frequency feels comfortable. You could use the sound "im" (as in "chime"), or "ima," or any sound you wish. Fifteen to thirty minutes of this, once or twice a day, can yield some interesting effects.

After a few thousand hours (no kidding) of this kind of meditation, it became clear to me what was happening. Essentially the chatter stops when you have some place to put your attention. The mantra became the attention-grabber. Now, you might ask, why in the world did you spend so much time learning how to stop your chatter? My answer is that the experience of being awake without any stuff going on in your head is pretty nice. Meditators often call it "transcendence," meaning simply that they rise above the normal chatter and feel peaceful. There are plenty of favorable physiological effects that have been well documented. They include reduced blood pressure, improved immunological responses, better ability to concentrate on work and study. There is no doubt that quieting the mind is good for you.

But it also feels good. While reading these pages, you have probably more or less been concentrating on the messages and periodically having a few private thoughts along the way. You have been judging whether you like what you are reading, how it applies, how you agree or disagree—whatever. You and I have been on this little journey together. But, if you close your eyes for a minute, you'll see that your thoughts take off on their own. Earlier we labeled those thoughts chatter. We said they are generated by the meta-level function of your brain. They judge, they produce the sense of self, they are the source and the conscious experience of emotion.

Now, imagine these thoughts stopping. You're still awake. But there are no thoughts. What's left? What is consciousness without thought? That's an experience of closed-eye meditation. When your eyes are open and you are engaged in activity, then it's a very pleasurable engagement. When your eyes are closed and you are experiencing no thoughts, you fill with joy. If you let yourself focus too much on that joy, it fades. The more you direct your attention to it, the more it fades. The ideal experience is to just experience.

Joyful Egolessness

As indicated, there are plenty of other meditation techniques that will take you to conscious chatterlessness. For some people, prayer delivers them to that place. Others use sutras: meaningful sounds that are used in ways similar to mantras. Yoga is a means to the same end. They all reduce to the same effect: the elimination of a sense of ego or self.

The lingering effects on your consciousness of this experience of transcendence can be pretty amazing as well. Under certain circumstances, such as prolonged transcendence, or repeated transcendence, or the right physical environment, or the purging of certain emotional baggage, you can go about your business while having this sense of joy accompany you. It dissolves when you admire it, but you can learn to balance your attention on real-world stuff while sustaining a kind of joyful egolessness.

There is always pain underneath ego. I have referred to it in various ways, as insecurity, fear, or feelings of emptiness. When we are not focused on the object-level or otherwise transcended through some meditative-like process, we become subject to all sorts of angst-ridden experiences. We judge, we blame, we hide, we worry, we take control, or we get panicky. We experience ourselves as a singularity that thinks it's special in some way.

But good news! We can transcend this dynamic and leave our symptoms behind. It's not that we can permanently exit from the meta-level paradigm. I have never met anyone who is free of the impulse to, for example, feel hurt. This thing called "mental health" comes in fits and starts, and in degrees. Without the meta-level doing its job, we wouldn't be humans.

So we have been blessed and we have been cursed. We are cursed because we have this illusion-promoting program that drives us to what Buddhists call a life of suffering. We are blessed because, with effort, we can periodically transcend our suffering and be more true to ourselves.

Visualize yourself living a willful, compassionate, and authentic life, making peace with your fears, relaxing your judgments, staying focused on the facts. Visualize the possibility of the true you, insecurities transcended, facing the future with presence of mind.

Now imagine your workplace with other people taking this path as well: people working together with commitment, ego-free communication, and compassion, with joy infused in task orientation as they reach synergies peacefully together.

Such a life—for you and the people you work with—is not only desirable, it is also quite achievable. And achieving it would be a beautiful thing.

Bibliography

Assagioli, Roberto. *The Act of Will.* New York: Penguin Books, 1974.

Branden, Nathaniel. *The Psychology of Self-Esteem.* New York: Bantam Books, 1969.

Csikszentmihalyi, Mihaly. *Flow: The Psychology of Optimal Experience.* New York: Harper Perennial, 1991.

Damasio, Antonio R. *Descartes' Error: Emotion, Reason, and the Human Brain.* New York: Grosset/Putnam, 1994.

Dennett, Daniel C. *Consciousness Explained.* New York: Little, Brown, 1991.

Ellis, Albert and Robert A. Harper. *A New Guide to Rational Living.* North Hollywood, Calif.: Wilshire Book Company, 1975.

Epstein, Mark. *Thoughts Without a Thinker.* New York: Basic Books, 1995.

Ferrucci, Piero. *What We May Be.* New York: Jeremy P. Tarcher, 1982.

Fromm, Erich. *The Art of Loving.* New York: Harper Perennial, 2000.

Goleman, Daniel. *Emotional Intelligence.* New York: Bantam Books, 1995.

Hanh, Thich Nhat. *The Miracle of Mindfulness: An Introduction to the Practice of Meditation.* Boston: Beacon Press, 1999.

Helmstetter, Shad. *What to Say When You Talk to Your Self.* New York: Pocket Books, 1986.

James, William. *The Principles of Psychology, Volume One.* Mineola, N.Y.: Dover Publications, 1950.

Jaynes, Julian. *The Origin of Consciousness in the Breakdown of the Bicameral Mind.* Boston: Houghton Mifflin, 1990.

Keyes, Ken Jr. *Handbook to Higher Consciousness.* Coos Bay, Ore.: Love Line Books, 1975.

Maslow, Abraham H. *Motivation and Personality,* 2nd ed. New York: Harper & Row, 1954.

Norretranders, Tor. *The User Illusion.* New York: Penguin Books, 1998.

Ornstein, Robert. *The Roots of the Self.* San Francisco: HarperSanFrancisco, 1993.

Peck, M. Scott. *The Road Less Traveled and Beyond: Spiritual Growth in an Age of Anxiety.* New York: Simon & Schuster, 1997.

Pert, Candace B. *Molecules of Emotion.* New York: Scribner, 1997.

Rogers, Carl R. *On Becoming a Person.* Boston: Houghton Mifflin, 1961.

Rogers, Carl R. *A Way of Being.* Boston: Houghton Mifflin, 1980.

Sartre, Jean-Paul. *Being and Nothingness.* New York: Washington Square Press, 1966.

Seligman, Martin E. P. *Learned Optimism: How to Change Your Mind and Your Life.* New York: Pocket Books, 1992.

Wegner, Daniel M. *White Bears and Other Unwanted Thoughts: Suppression, Obsession and the Psychology of Mental Control.* New York: Guilford Publications, 1994.

Wilber, Ken. *A Brief History of Everything.* Boston: Shambhala, 1996.

Index